WAITING
While Dating

WAITING While Dating

CHRISTIAN COUPLES WHO KEPT GOD FIRST FROM COURTSHIP TO MARRIAGE

LINDSEY HOLDER

AMBASSADOR INTERNATIONAL
GREENVILLE, SOUTH CAROLINA & BELFAST, NORTHERN IRELAND

www.ambassador-international.com

Waiting While Dating

Christian Couples Who Kept God First
From Courtship to Marriage

ISBN: 978-1-62020-563-1
eISBN: 978-1-62020-494-8

Cover Design and Page Layout by Hannah Nichols
eBook Conversion by Anna Riebe Raats

AMBASSADOR INTERNATIONAL
Emerald House
411 University Ridge, Suite B14
Greenville, SC 29601, USA
www.ambassador-international.com

AMBASSADOR BOOKS
The Mount
2 Woodstock Link
Belfast, BT6 8DD, Northern Ireland, UK
www.ambassadormedia.co.uk

The colophon is a trademark of Ambassador

DEDICATION

Dedicated to You, Lord. You sought me out to be a voice for others. After my hurts, protests, and anger, You molded me into a woman who has grown toward You in unimaginable ways. You never cease to bewilder me, Your love is endless, Your grace abounds for me, and Your kindness overwhelms me. I see clearly how every piece of my life has fallen into place, even when I got the puzzle out of order. Your wisdom knew I was going to do that. Thank You. I humbly look forward to what will happen next.

This book is dedicated to *your* new beginnings, grace, discovering biblical wisdom, growing closer to our Heavenly Father, trusting He knows best, overcoming obstacles, and discovering a beautiful lit path ahead for your future.

It is also dedicated to Kerry H. Thank you for your guidance, your counsel, and showing me what a Proverbs 31 woman looks like and the beauty and gift of waiting for a godly man. You made a tremendous impact on my life; I thank you.

To my parents: thank you for showing me the strength of a Christian couple who has endured the trials of life and weathered every challenge together.

To my sister: you are my daily advisor and confidant. How grateful I am to have you in my life.

The book is dedicated to December 2012, the month and year God spoke to me and drew me to Himself. Little did I know that You would take me through painful trials, test my endurance, and reveal unforeseen truth, sinfulness, and brokenness. This book is also dedicated to what came out of my trials: grace, light, wisdom, mercy, joy, forgiveness, redemption, friendships, strength, and, most importantly, the lesson of putting God first.

ACKNOWLEDGMENTS

An overwhelming thank you to the six couples who took time out of their lives to sit down with me and share their path to meeting their spouses. What an incredible honor to know you and hear your stories. Every couple had a different way of meeting and courting, but the one common factor they had was seeking this through God's way. Thank you for personally showing me the strengths and godly mindset of both the male and female perspective.

Thank you to Grace Church for being an abundant source of tools, resources, staff, community, leadership, wisdom, encouragement, strength, and support. A special thank you to Matt Williams and Chrystie Cole for meeting with me and having a *significant* impact on this book. I am grateful for a church that speaks about topics often overlooked and gives me honest answers when I'm seeking truth. Thank you for leading not only our youth but followers of Christ of all ages so that we may continually grow in His strength and always strive to seek God's best.

CONTENTS

INTRODUCTION

I have been through the emotional pain of a divorce, but as of this writing have never been married.

How is that possible? Simple: I concentrated on my personal desires rather than God's instruction clearly laid out in His Word. He is not to be argued with, half listened to, or disputed against. You do not doubt God's direction. There is no option of partially obeying the Lord without bearing the consequences of shame and separation. Partial faithfulness is non-existent. It is one way to believe God's Word, and it is another to obey it. It is one way to believe God's Word and another to *admit* what you are actually doing.

The Lord expects us to do what He says without debate. God's requirements are timeless, with no bearing on age or our past. It is disheartening when we take matters into our own hands and allow relationships to occur and develop that were not selected by God. How vital to know God has a plan for us and has not forgotten us. Trust His guidance and rely on His promises. He expects us to seek and find, but He will never forget or forsake us during our journey.

A few of the rewards of following His Word? Less pain, fewer regrets, and the most surprising? Fewer memories. You may be forgiven, but the memories remain as a reminder of your disobedience and lack of discipline and judgment. In a spontaneous heated moment, an easy, feel-good choice seems effortless to make. Did you stop and think if that relationship did not work out? In that moment everything can appear wonderful, and it is easy to "live in the moment" and see where it goes. But in the end, the "moment(s)" will last forever, imprinted on your heart. It will also affect future moments with the husband or wife God has planned for you.

This relates to emotional, physical, and spiritual oversharing before it's time.

In today's culture we plan and prepare for our future with education, training, and working diligently to be successful in our business ventures and career. We thirst for knowledge, crave to be the best, and chip at it every day to be the guru in our field. But in relationships, we tend to fail ourselves so easily. We allow our hearts to be carefree, not planning for our heart's future, for our emotional health, for the memories we make. We easily connect, giving so much of ourselves before it is time without truly understanding who we are giving that to and without having received an ordained commitment of marriage in return. Why are the most precious gifts given so freely?

Yes, forgiveness and redemption are wonderful. Thank you God for allowing us countless chances to strive for obedience and faithfulness. What if you gave yourself a chance to be faithful? How freeing would that be?

If this is on the man's end, Chrystie Cole points out in *Redeeming Sexuality,* "By engaging in sex prior to marriage, you are *not* encouraging him to be a man and take responsibility for your relationship. On the contrary, you enable him to remain a boy."

Matt Williams states in *Eden Derailed,* "Intimacy flourishes in the content of commitment." Chrystie Cole responds, "This is true of relational intimacy, emotional intimacy, and sexual intimacy."

So what does that look like? Just as your future is planned, how is your future heart planned? God is clear in His answers: you follow His Word.

In the Bible, there isn't anything listed besides marriage and un-marriage. That's it, no in between—no gray area. It is simple: you are not married to this person, so therefore do not do things married people do. Period.

What lie are you telling yourself? If you are unable to stand in front of God Himself and be proud of your actions, then there is your answer. If He would not have approved it, then anything else is just an excuse you are telling yourself.

So how is that established? It's easy to read and be clear on paper prior to reality. To get to know someone requires you to share gradually to establish if indeed *they are* that marriage partner. What questions do you ask your potential partner and when? What boundaries do you set? At what point in the relationship do you bring Christ into it? What is over the limit and appropriate?

As you study His Word, you will find God provides you all of the wisdom you need to find the qualities and characteristics of a marriage partner. But He expects you to study His Word, obey His Word, and have a faithful heart in the interim. Through Scripture, God provides the wisdom on what type of character, values, and morals to seek in a person: someone not in anger, equally yoked, etc.

In reality, on a real date, when chemistry is involved, you are fighting off your naturally produced endorphins and endless supply of dopamine. So while your brain wants to know all of these answers to specific questions, your eyes are bewildered by attractive features and you are fighting the urge to get closer, faster. You are responding naturally; the attraction is there. How are you supposed to keep it together and composed?

Boundaries and a plan.

If clear boundaries and a plan are set from the start, both partners can hold each other accountable. There is a catch: *both* partners *have* to be on the *same* page about the boundaries. If your partner pressures you or makes you feel guilty for keeping to those boundaries, you need to question their real motives and intentions. The ultimate goal should be marriage. No need to pursue someone unless you are ready to commit to that goal. Otherwise, you are merely using that person to meet your own selfish desires. Even God has boundaries and allows consequences when they are crossed. He is clear.

False reasons to engage in physical intimacy before marriage? Among others, I have heard these lies on why their partner or their selves "approved" the intimacy. Notice they are man-made, not ordained by God:

- It's not like you are a virgin.
- I'm not your first, so what's the big deal?
- I don't want to marry someone without knowing what it will be like.

- It's how I show I love someone.
- It makes me feel loved.
- Those commandments applied to those back then; it's outdated now. They were so young when they married.
- Those might apply to teenagers. We are adults.
- I need to have my needs met. (Note: These are not needs; they are desires.)

Examples of boundaries in dating? Details. My goal in writing this was to discover a few concrete details on how six Christian-based couples did just that. They got to know each other with an eye toward marriage. Note that all couples were dating while the ultimate goal was marriage. Was it hard? Absolutely. Were they wildly attracted to each other? Yes. They were not unlike most dating people; they all had the same raging desires. If they didn't, that would be a problem since physical oneness is an essential part of marriage. But they also courted with faithfulness and took the time to ask and answer hard questions and be on the same page physically, spiritually, and emotionally. It takes work on both parties with both equally open to doing the work prior to the commitment. Relationships are work, but anything worth having is work. Isn't work worth having? The key is to wait for the ultimate partner who will do the work with you. As Andy Stanley says, "Every kiss is a part of your permanent story." So make it a story you will be proud to tell.

A final note: Of course more questions could be asked, but the questions in this book are a good base to get your mind and heart in shape for how you will behave during your courtship.

Hopefully it will reduce your heartache (as that is inevitable) along the way.

Put Christ first in your relationship. Live out emotional, spiritual, and sexual integrity in your dating relationship to give you a strong foundation into your marriage.

Give yourself a chance to find the person willing to serve in the trenches with you.

Restore your relationship with your Father first and focus on His Word. The rest will fall into place. Marriage is messy, complicated, and downright dirty at times. Give yourself a chance to find the person willing to serve in the trenches with you.

MOM AND DAD: [BACK IN THOSE DAYS]

MEET COUPLE ONE: MOM AND DAD

AGES WHEN MARRIED:

Both were 21

LENGTH DATED:

7 months

LENGTH ENGAGED:

8 months

HOW LONG MARRIED NOW:

48 years

HOW THEY MET:

My father's sister suggested my mother was a nice girl and from a nice family. My aunt thought my father should ask my mother out since he was home from college for the summer.

Mom and I were sitting at Applebee's, dining on one of their lighter fare selections as we seem to always be trying the latest low-calorie trend. As we waited for our meal, I thought I would tell her about my new book and my vision for it. As I listed a few couples I thought would be ideal for the book, Mom stopped me and said something I never expected: "Well, what about your father and I? You know, *we* could be in the book."

That thought had never occurred to me. I felt a little disappointed in myself that I had never considered my parents. Once my mom mentioned the idea, it dawned on me—of course they should be in the book! It was the perfect fit, especially for me. What other couple had I been given a front row seat to personally witness the ups and downs, the trials of marriage, the healings of marriage, the bonds that one spouse can have for another? I have watched my dad court my mom my entire life. He always brings her a dessert (in fact, these days she will get upset if he doesn't), have a random, thoughtful card at her chair at dinner, and Friday night has been date night for as long as I can remember.

It is fascinating to me that even after forty-eight years of marriage, they still have questions for one another, their quirks still drive each other crazy, and they talk to each other a ridiculous amount during the day. It amazes me there is not a loss for words. They are NOT that quiet couple at the dinner table that stare at their food in silence. There has always, *always* been something to chat about, dispute about, story tell, or laugh about. So I guess that is what good friends do; they always want that person by their side, and their friendship is a never ending conversation. Sometimes their conversations are louder than others, but they are always ongoing, entertaining, and filled with love.

After observing these years of my parents' marriage, it was a must to interview them and find out how the beginnings all came about. It was time I learned some history and details about my folks.

PART I - ATTRACTION

What attracted you to this person in the beginning?

My dad said, "She was very pretty and available." For the record, this is not the romantic serenade I had imagined. My mom, in return, liked my dad because he was in church and had a nice family. She liked how he believed the same as she did. She said, "His family was a lot like mine, and I wanted to marry someone that acted like my daddy." It's worth noting that Mom also came back saying, "I also liked that he was tall and had dark brown eyes." Oh goodness. The giggles started to kick in with my parents as they started down memory lane after the first question.

What characteristics were you looking for in your future partner?

Dad said Mom was someone that was from a good, stable family that would be compatible. Mom agreed and felt the same way about Dad.

Did he automatically lead from the start of contact? What did that look like (from the woman's perspective)?

He made all the moves. If he had not called, that would have been the end of it. Mom would have not pursued him. He called her, made all the plans, and always paid for her.

What form of communication had been your primary one? Did you talk about if you prefer to text, see each other, or talk on the phone?

Both agreed they communicated both by phone and in person. Dad also said he would take her for sweet tea and hushpuppies at the drive-thru after church, occasionally ice cream, and then take her home. I asked my dad if he walked my mom to the front door after a date. He replied, *"Of course,* I wanted to get my sugar."

My mom said my dad knew he would see her in church on Sunday morning and Sunday night. My mom would sing in the choir on Sunday nights so she would sit with him after she came down from the choir.

When into the relationship did you discuss your intentions and expectations for the relationship? Who brought it up?

Both my parents agreed that he did. Six weeks into the relationship, he asked my mom to go steady and wear his high school ring. She said no. He waited four more months and asked her again. She then said yes—emphatically.

When do you think you grew close to each other?

My dad was instantly infatuated with my mom. For my mom, she was ready when the four months came and he asked her to go steady.

When did you first say *I love you*? Did you have the intention at that point for marriage?

It was between months four and eight of dating for my dad, but he could not recall the exact moment. He had marriage on his mind after the first few dates. My mom could not recall when she told him she loved him first. She did, however, have the intention at that point for marriage.

At what point in the relationship did you "know" you desired each other as your marriage partner? What was it that made you know? Was it a feeling or was something done?

My dad felt my mom was "the one" about the second date. My mom was more cautious but felt he was "the one" after several months.

Did you discuss what love language you responded to? When did you start acting upon that (e.g., cards that expressed your emotion, acts of kindness, cooking for one another etc.)? Was this done before, during, or after the engagement?

Both exchanged Valentine, birthday, Christmas, and the occasional "sweetheart" cards. My father would mail them to her. They did not discuss an actual love language. There was no cooking for each other as they both lived at home with their parents.

Do you feel waiting for sexual intimacy sped up the dating process?

Both unanimously said no.

How hard was it to maintain the commitment before sexual intimacy?

For them, waiting wasn't hard at all. It was the common understanding to wait.

Did you discuss your sexual past or past partners, if any? When did you start to discuss this?

My dad said no, as there was no need. He knew how she was raised and who she had dated in the past. He just knew. Mom also said no and pretty much gave the same answer. She also knew who he was and how he was raised.

PART II - BOUNDARIES AND ACCOUNTABILITY

Going into these questions with my parents made me both a little squeamish and curious at the same time. Asking your dad how long he waited "to make a move" on Mom is a bit uncomfortable. On the other hand, I was eager to know both how my dad respected my mother as well as how my mother required him to treat her. I enjoyed learning about their hush puppy outings, how my grandmother kept them in check and that old-fashioned cards are hard to beat. It surprised me that certain questions were never brought up or discussed, but at the same time it impressed me how well they kept their boundaries and clarity in the relationship.

Describe your first date:

They went on a double date to a rhythm and blues beach music club with live entertainers, which was apparently something considered out of the ordinary back then.

Did you establish boundaries from the get go? Who led that conversation?

No, there was no discussion. They just knew and had their own personal boundaries and moral code.

What boundaries did you create? Did you have the same boundaries?

Yes, they both had the same boundaries.

How did you hold each other accountable to those boundaries?

Living with their parents made a difference. Also her mother never went to sleep until my mom came

Asking your dad how long he waited "to make a move" on Mom is a bit uncomfortable.

home. Her curfew was midnight. My mother said every time she would come home, her mother always seemed to have to go to the bathroom down the hall at that exact time and asked her how her night had been. It was my grandmother's way of checking up on my mom.

They both went to the same church and held the same church beliefs. The weekly church sermons also held them accountable.

When did you start holding hands? What date was your first kiss?

They held hands on the second date and had their first kiss on either the third or fourth date.

How did you control your sexual desires for each other? Did you discuss the difficulty of controlling your desire for each other?

They did not discuss their desires; they knew they desired each other. They both used personal restraint to control those desires.

Was this a local or long-distance relationship?

It was a local relationship.

Did you ever spend the night at each other's house? Was this in the same bed? Were there other people in the house at the time? What was the situation?

No, they never spent the night at each other's house.

Did you mainly do daytime dates? Did you do more group or one-on-one dating? Any overnight trips?

Mainly it was evening, one-on-one dates. He would take her to a drive-in movie or would come and sit on the front porch swing at night. My dad did not like group dates; he did not want to share her with anyone. He wanted her attention focused on him. There were no overnight trips.

At what point did you have a relationship and open discussions with his family, including seeing you involved as a part of the future family unit?

This happened only for my dad when he asked for her hand in marriage. They had dinner every Sunday at one of their parents' houses, so they were actively involved in each other's families. My dad also went on a camping trip with my mother's family so was well known with her family.

Did you have a close person in your life who held you accountable, truly had your best interest in mind, and gave you advice?

No, but having a curfew, being a part of the church together, and knowing each other's family helped them with accountability.

PART III - A CHRIST-CENTERED RELATIONSHIP

I knew my parents met at church, but learning how *much* time they spent together at church was new to me. I had pictured in my mind my mom and dad hanging out on Sunday a few times, seeing each other at service, or attending a congregation dinner here and there. Hearing the details of their church life and finding out how involved they were, made all of the other chapters and answers fall into place

> A great admiration on what a Christ-centered relationship looks like was right in front of me the whole time. I just needed to open my eyes and watch.

for me. They had surrounded themselves with faith and people who shared their morals and values. Christ was always at the center of their relationship, so a lot of the boundary questions seemed to answer themselves. My parents raised the bar for me after knowing their answers and listening to their dating stories. A great admiration on what a Christ-centered relationship looks like was right in front of me the whole time. I just needed to open my eyes and watch.

The first time you shared a meal; did he offer to bless the meal?

Yes, he said the blessing at every meal.

Were you raised with the same religious backgrounds and values?

Yes, they had exactly the same backgrounds and values.

Did you come from the same faith or denomination?

Yes, they are both Baptist.

Did you attend the same church when you met? If not, whose church did you start attending and when did you start attending together?

Yes. Both went to the same church. They really didn't have a choice as both sets of parents went to the same church.

When did you start praying together?

They said the blessing and prayed communally at church. They started praying together only after their engagement.

Did you serve together while you were dating? Were they the same roles?

No, they did not serve together. (Mom sang in the choir, and Dad was an usher sometimes.)

Did you establish a mentor relationship with other strong Christian married couples while dating?

They didn't have any mentor relationships outside of their parents.

Did you do any type of workbook or study together? If so, when was this into the relationship? Did you think this was valuable?

No, they didn't complete any type of workbook.

Did you participate in premarital counseling after engagement?

No premarital counseling was done. They spoke to their preacher for about one hour regarding marital responsibilities. This occurred about thirty days prior to their marriage.

Were you a part of a study or Bible group? If so, when was this into the relationship?

Yes, they went to a Bible class on Sunday nights, which they both attended even prior to dating each other.

Were you a part of a weekly community group? If so, when was this into the relationship?

No, but they had Sunday school, Wednesday night prayer meeting, and church on Sunday night.

Did you discuss what religion would look like in your family (e.g., go to church weekly or more than weekly; involvement of church in daily life and finances; if children would go to Christian schooling, etc.)?

No, it was an understood attitude that they would continue church after marriage.

When into the relationship did you discuss any obstacles or addictions that you needed to overcome (finances, anger, abuse, pornography, alcoholism, gambling, etc.)? Was the elimination of these addictions expected? How were these problems resolved?

There were never any issues, and they did not discuss this.

PART IV - DAILY LIFE

Surprisingly, my parents spent a great deal of time together early into their relationship. I thought my dad would have taken it slow and played it cool, but he desired my mom and was not going to let her get away. He pursued her with persistence and a plan. In these days of "*I need my space* and *independence*," learning how much quality time my parents spent alone and with each other's families was refreshing. It allowed my parents to get to know each other, finding out about each other's personality and character through quality time. You can hide only so much from someone for so long, and learning of their daily communication and frequent visits won me over. Their interview not only opened my eyes to how well my parents got to know each other before marriage but also made me realize how involved both sets of my grandparents were. Both sides of my family embraced my parents, welcomed them into their homes, and had a place at the dinner table for both of them.

Through hospitality and generosity, my grandparents played a large part in setting my parents' boundaries without speaking a word.

Did you speak daily, early into the relationship? How long were your conversations at the beginning? When did this increase to a daily occurrence?

Yes, they spoke at least every day by phone. Each time they talked, it lasted one to two hours. They also saw each other three to four times a week.

What form of communication did you mainly use? How long were your conversations typically? Very quick and general or more in-depth, longer ones. How did your communication change as your relationship grew?

Social media did not exist back then. They mainly talked in person.

Dad sent Mom cards in the mail. Most of their conversations were deep, and the communication was constant; it did not change.

How many times a week did you see each other?

They saw each other between three and four times a week.

When did you meet each other's core group of friends?

They already knew each other's friends.

Did you discuss what type of movies to watch together? How did you handle it when one partner was uncomfortable with the content of the movie? What about TV shows, magazines, Internet activity?

Mom usually picked out the movie and Dad paid. Back then, there was generally only one movie showing at one time. In addition, those movie options were not mainstream at that time. There was no Internet back then.

Did you go to each other's house? When watching movies or TV, did you lie down side by side, sit up right, or on separate couches?

Yes, they went to each other's house. They typically sat side by side and held hands.

Did you have other friends of the opposite sex while dating? Did you agree that as you became more intimately involved, those relationships would need to change? How did you handle that? When into the relationship was this? How were those relationships changed?

No, neither one had friends of the opposite sex.

What were your boundaries with the opposite sex (e.g., no lunch alone, no private phone calls, etc.)?

There were no boundaries because there were no other relationships.

Did you establish to set an open and safe conversation when one partner felt the other partner crossed the line with the opposite sex or made them feel uncomfortable?

No, as that never happened.

PART V - SOCIAL MEDIA BOUNDARIES, EXPECTATIONS, AND ACCOUNTABILITY

Envisioning my mom and dad chatting online when they first met seems so far beyond unimaginable from nowadays. It also would be hysterical. My mom would most likely wink at the wrong person, and my dad would probably accidentally delete my mom's profile. It would be a mess. God knew what He was doing to have them meet when they did. Social media has not been an issue with them, and it was nice to hear that. I have made myself very prevalent on social media, and with that comes great responsibility and accountability that I have to accept. Hearing their answers on openness and honesty in those areas is exactly what I was hoping they would say. I look forward to seeking those same traits in a future spouse.

How did you keep each other accountable with social media while dating? Did this change after you were married?

They did not have social media or the Internet until much later in their marriage. Now, they do have each other's passwords to any account if desired to hold each other accountable.

Did you discuss how you would handle your social media interactions and accounts including, but not limited to, emails, Facebook, Twitter, and Instagram while dating? If so, when into the relationship was this?

This didn't apply until long after they were married. They are free to check any social media platform and emails if desired.

Did you keep each other accountable on web browsing and viewing while dating? If you found something that made you feel uncomfortable, did you have open communication lines with your partner? What about after marriage?

This was not an issue during dating as they did not have the Internet. After marriage, both of them use the same computer in the main living room and they each have access to the other's passwords. They have an open communication and ask each other any questions if needed.

FINAL THOUGHTS FROM MOM AND DAD

"We were ready to commit to a permanent relationship when we met. It was God who brought us together, and everything that followed is a result of His plan. God always provides, whether it is a relationship, family, or keeping us well and away from harm. In Genesis 17:16 God gave Sarah not only a son but made her the mother of the nation of Israel long after she should have been too old to have children. In 1 Kings 17 God hid and provided Elijah with food and drink during a drought that lasted several years so he could continue being His prophet. God has a plan for all of us, and if we trust Him, He will be faithful and bring to us only His best."

God has a plan for all of us, and if we trust Him, He will be faithful and bring to us only His best.

It seemed so simple back then. You liked a girl, you knew her family, and you asked her out. You spent time with her family and got to know them. During my parents' time, there were fewer broken marriages, so most of *their* friends' parents were still together, and relationships just seemed easier. Having so many options now, in a time where you can swipe left or right based on if you like someone's hair or their killer smile, may result in the man having less of an opportunity to lead. Why should he make the effort to connect and pursue a girl in church when he can wink at one online? The rejection will be over in an instant, without seeing the sting on her face. But what if he wasn't rejected, or what if she was worth the chance to speak to her? I know so many amazing single gals sitting on that church bench, waiting for that nice guy to walk up to them and say, "Good morning." Listening to my parents' story is bittersweet to me. It's an era, a way of thinking, that is a rare find nowadays. Maybe that can change. Maybe we *can* have some of those good ol' days back in a simpler time. Maybe I will start to hear more stories of "good mornings" being said to those gals on Sundays. Just maybe. That would be nice.

DISCUSSION QUESTIONS

- How much quality time during the week do you think is needed to get to know a potential spouse on a deeper level?
- What type of communication do you generally prefer: in-person conversations, longer phone calls, or short bursts of texts throughout the day? What type of communication does he or she prefer?
- Do you desire a more traditional courtship like this couple shared, or a more modern type of relationship?
- How involved would you like the family of your potential mate to be?

PATRICK AND KATHRYN: [ALMOST 30]

MEET PATRICK AND KATHRYN:

AGES WHEN MARRIED:

Him: 27; Her: 29

LENGTH DATED:

12 months

LENGTH ENGAGED:

5 months

HOW LONG MARRIED NOW:

11 months

HOW THEY MET:

They met through mutual friends, a family for whom she was babysitting while pursuing her photography career. She had been in two unhealthy relationships previously and was angry at God. They were supposedly "Christian guys," and she did not need to date anyone after that for a while. He was briefly dating another woman at that time. They had been hearing about each other for about eight months, and then the family she was babysitting for arranged them to meet at a dinner. A week later, he asked her out.

Owning a small business in the spa industry allows me to meet the most incredible women. Kathryn is one of them. She had been a client for a couple of years and even though I saw her in small bits at a time, they were frequent for a while. I enjoyed listening to her life happenings, as she was always busy and bustling. Her photography business was getting larger by the minute, so she had a sharp mind and was gifted with her talents. Capturing weddings was one of her specialties. It was always interesting for me to observe how a woman dealt with another woman's happiest moments of life while she herself desired the same in her heart. I connected with Kathryn as I also dealt with brides on a daily basis, getting them ready for their big day as I waited patiently for my wedding day to come and desired mine equally as much.

Kathryn would talk about a guy here and there, and we shared in common how few and far in between the good ones were to come. It was about a year and a half of swapping our stories back and forth and honestly sharing pure frustration at not finding a match.

Then one day, she seemed different. A ray of confidence seemed to shine as it never had before, and she carried herself with an abundance of smiles. Ahh! A new guy was in the picture.

We chatted briefly each time I saw her, and I would ask a little more about the relationship. At the beginning, she was reserved, and I could tell it was not because she wasn't sure if she liked him or not. No, this time it was different. This time she held back as she knew she liked him to the point where she needed to guard her heart until the time was right.

Each time I saw Kathryn on my calendar, I would get excited to hear what she and her new boyfriend had been up to, to learn how it was going, and to ask her all types of questions. It was probably a bit too much interrogation, but I couldn't help myself. The way she would describe him and tell me about the things he would do for her renewed my hope that he might be the one for her. I loved to hear how much of a gentleman he was, and his actions showed how he cherished her.

The day Kathryn came in and waved her hand that sparkled from her engagement ring was a happier moment for me than she knows. I knew how trendy, modern, and cool this couple was, so hearing the wooing of her with old-fashioned ways gave me a tinge of happiness and hope that old-time manners were still going on out there in the dating world, even in my hometown.

What attracted you to this person in the beginning?

Patrick saw a picture of her and thought she was pretty. Kathryn also had a good job, liked kids, and was fun and very independent. She also saw a picture of him and thought he was really cute. She was attracted to the fact that he had a job, loved Jesus, and loved kids.

What characteristics were you looking for in your future partner?

He needed an independent woman—he wanted her to rely on herself with God, had her friends, and wasn't clingy or needy. He wanted someone who he was able to have fun with, liked to be around people, and wasn't afraid to tell you what she was thinking.

She was not going to date just to date. She liked how it was not a game to him, and he did not want to waste her time—she was looking for someone to spend the rest of her life with. She wanted someone to lead her but allow her to have her independence, someone to confide in and have assurance in. Qualities that her father had are what she was looking for in a man. She desired someone who was driven, kind, and sensitive—all the things she was not. She liked how he reminded her to be gentle, and she didn't feel the need to be strong all the time.

Did he automatically lead from the start of contact? What did that look like? (woman's perspective)

Oh, yeah, Patrick called and asked Kathryn out. They went on a date the next day as she was gone the day after that for work. He came by her house to pick her up (they hung out two times in a large group prior to that), walked her to her door, opened her car door, and even asked her out again. He never left her hanging or made her guess if there was a next time. He always shared his intentions and let her know where the relationship was going.

What form of communication had been your primary one? Did you talk about if you prefer to text, see each other, or talk on the phone?

When they did not see each other, they would randomly text each other as a surprise. On the nights they did not have a date they would talk on the phone, and he would call her before bed to say goodnight.

When into the relationship did you discuss your intentions and expectations for the relationship? Who brought it up?

On the fourth date, he brought it up. They went to go cut down a Christmas tree and had a long drive. She talked about how nervous she was about meeting his parents and he assured her it would be fine. On the drive they talked about past relationships. They also talked about how they were having fun dating and wanted to keep on that path and weren't dating just to date. He let her know he would not be spending that much time with her if it was not intentional. (During the interview, he mentioned he would not be spending that much money either! He had enough friends to go to dinner with.)

When do you think you grew close to her? To him?

Neither was sure if there was a specific time, but it was around the four-month point in their relationship. In Patrick's past relationships, he did not enjoy their families as much as he did Kathryn's, and he knew you also "marry into the family." He liked that she wasn't too whiny and complaining. She could pick herself up and keep going.

When he went to Israel for a church trip, it was the first time Kathryn missed him. Her heart hurt as he was across the world. Her past relationships were long distance, and she did not see them sometimes for a month at a time and was fine with that. With Patrick, it was the first time her heart physically ached, and she wanted to see him every day.

When did you first say *I love you*? Did you have the intention at that point for marriage?

Patrick told Kathryn he loved her six months into the relationship, a day before his birthday. Yes, he thinks that was the thought process. It was an ongoing conversation. She told him she loved him back.

At what point in the relationship did you "know" you desired each other as your marriage partner? What was it that made you know? Was it a feeling or was something done?

For him it was seven months into the relationship, right after they talked about it. They both wanted someone they would enjoy their time together with. He liked how she was a lot of fun. It was more of a feeling—like if he was going to hang out with someone it would be with her.

Around month four to five, she knew she wanted to be with him all the time. It was not one specific thing that triggered her mind. Kathryn didn't think there was just "one" person but knew Patrick was everything she had wanted and that he was worth working on. They had the same goals and desires for how they wanted their family to be. They were both raised in two loving families and could relate to that. She also liked how she got along with his parents.

Did you discuss what love language you responded to? When did you start acting upon that (e.g., cards that expressed your emotion, acts of kindness, cooking for one another etc.)? Was this done before, during, or after the engagement?

During a relationship series at their church the preacher talked about the five love relationships. When dating, both of them had the same love language, which included quality time and physical touch. She was praying every day that he would not break up with her. During the sermon series it talked about ways to better serve your partner—including encouragement. The series made her aware of what she needed to do more of.

Do you feel waiting for sexual intimacy sped up the dating process?

Yes, that and age. He had a pretty clear picture of what he was looking for.

How hard was it maintaining the commitment before intimacy?

It was very tough. Patrick and Kathryn had to set boundaries. When you can only kiss or make-out, it's very hard.

Did you discuss your sexual past or past partners, if any? When did you start to discuss this?

Yes, they did. They talked about that early on within the first two months and were dating seriously at that point.

PART II - BOUNDARIES AND ACCOUNTABILITY

Interviewing Kathryn was interesting to me because I always thought she was a confident woman. Hearing her alongside Patrick after their marriage, she was even more so, but at the same time, she was offering a more generous heart. A different type of security was there, one that she had been holding back and waiting for until she found it in her husband. The trust that she had been looking for was finally given to her, allowing her to open up and give a bar-none answer to everything. It was apparent that, through God, Patrick's godly traits helped close up the scars from her past and renewed her trust again in men. It was comforting for me to witness and hear her talk, as I knew one day my scars could be spackled over by trust with the right man if I put God first to bring us together just as she had.

Describe your first date:

Patrick called Kathryn and asked her out. He said he would pick her up at 6pm and asked for her address. They went to a local restaurant downtown where he had planned the date. He always had a plan, and she liked that. They talked until the restaurant closed, and at the end of the date he walked her to her door and gave her a side hug. He asked her out again that night. He was nervous about asking her out again because he thought she was having a miserable time. She seemed uncomfortable and guarded.

However, he had been talked to about her past by the friend that ended up officiating Patrick and Kathryn's wedding ceremony. The friend sat Patrick down and gave him clarity on where she was, about her brother's passing, and that there was going to be a lot of trust that had to be earned.

Did you establish boundaries from the get go? Who led that conversation?

Patrick led that conversation.

What boundaries did you create? Did you have the same boundaries?

Patrick did not go into Kathryn's house until the third or fourth date. When he dropped her off after a date, he would maybe give her a hug but his affirmation would be always asking her out for another date. They did not cuddle on the couch until around four months into the relationship. They would sit on the couch beside each other not even touching. She had a roommate, so they did not do a lot by themselves. They stayed out of each other's bedrooms and never stayed past 10pm. They made a conscious effort to leave at that time as they both had work the next day and both understood it was not to be argued about.

A lot of it was just understood. They spooned on the couch after engagement but then had to stop as the temptation was too great.

How did you hold each other accountable to those boundaries?

There was not a conversation about sex—it was the first time for both of them so it was just understood. They just did not do it.

When did you start holding hands? What date was your first kiss?

They held hands two months into the relationship, when they were official. They never held hands in public, it was usually while driving. Neither of them was a huge public affections person. He kissed her about one month into the relationship.

How did you control your sexual desires for each other? Did you discuss the difficulty of controlling your desire for each other?

They did not go into each other's bedrooms, they watched movies with the lights on, and there were people in the house, like her roommate. They did not sit on the couch for long amounts of time and stayed very active. They ran errands, cooked together, and were not home by themselves typically.

Was this a local or long-distance relationship? Can you offer advice on long-distance relationships (if so, did you stay at each other's place, how often do you see each other, should the man visit the woman more or equal, etc.)?

It was both as they lived thirty minutes apart. He thought traveling should be equal. They talked about it. When they first dated, he would drive to her. Then later on, they had a schedule for days they would see each other. On Mondays, Patrick would come to her house and they would cook together. On Tuesdays, Kathryn would go to his house and they would cook. Wednesdays he worked late so they talked on the phone. Thursday night it depended on what was going on, and they would sometimes hang out during the day as he got off earlier that day. Fridays they would see each other and on Saturdays she would go to his house. On Sundays they would go to church in the morning and then go to lunch together. He worked at the church so would bring her work there also and they would be together. Later on they would go to dinner with friends.

Did you ever spend the night at each other's house?

No.

Did you mainly do daytime dates? Did you do more group or one-on-one dating? Any overnight trips?

They were mainly one-on-one dates. They did hang out in groups, but they wanted to get to know each other. They went to the beach with a group of twelve married couples, and they stayed in separate rooms. They had overnight trips when they went to visit Patrick's parents out of town but never stayed in the same bed. The dates were both night and daytime dates.

At what point did you have a relationship and open discussions with his family, including seeing you involved as a part of the future family unit?

Both of them had separate conversations with their families. Patrick went to Kathryn's father after eight months to ask his permission to marry her. Her father said no because he wanted to get to know Patrick better. Of course, Patrick was taken back, and it was kind of an annoyance as he had the ring and an engagement party planned three days after, which he had to cancel. Her father asked him to wait three more months. He asked three months later, and her father approved.

She found out after they were engaged that her father initially said no to Patrick. She understood where her father was coming from. He was being protective of her as he saw how scarred she was from her past relationships, and Kathryn was thankful for her father's protection because it showed how much her father loved her. It also showed her future husband's patience and how driven he was.

Did you have a close person in your life that held you accountable, truly had your best interest in mind, and gave you advice?

Yes, they both had numerous people. Patrick had close guy friends and work relationships, and Kathryn had two of her best girlfriends involved.

PART III - A CHRIST-CENTERED RELATIONSHIP

Patrick and Kathryn impressed me with how much they surrounded themselves with their church family. They spent a great deal of time together in both group settings as well as individual dates. Patrick was in a leadership role at work, and he definitely spilled that over into his personal relationship as well. I admired the way he truly led Kathryn step by step, letting her know his intentions the entire way without false pretenses. Having mentors early in their relationship and spending time with them was a rarity I have heard about and thought very highly of this young couple making that decision. It showed they were being intentional in the direction toward marriage.

The first time you shared a meal did he offer to bless the meal?

Yes, on their first date.

Were you raised with the same religious backgrounds and values?

They were raised with the same values but different denominations.

Did you come from the same faith or denomination?

Patrick was raised Methodist and in college he changed to non-denominational, and Kathryn was raised Catholic and changed in college to non-denominational.

Did you attend the same church when you met? If not, whose church did you start attending, and when did you start attending together?

They both attended the same church before they knew each other. When they started dating each other, they would sit together at church. Since he worked at that church he would also have to work on Sundays. On those days, they would spend most of the day there and also make a point to sit with each other during service.

When did you start praying together?

They prayed at every meal. Patrick prayed for Kathryn by himself during his quiet time with the Lord, and she did the same. As a married couple they pray together every night.

Did you serve together while you were dating? Were they the same roles? (ex. both on coffee team or one serving in children's ministry and other serving as a greeter, etc.)

He served with the middle and high school students. She served in the nursery.

Did you establish a mentor relationship with other strong Christian married couples while dating?

Yes, they would go to dinner with their mentors and confide in them. After engagement, they asked for advice from their mentors.

Did you do any type of workbook or study together?

No.

Did you participate in premarital counseling after engagement?

Yes, they highly recommend it too. Their premarital counseling consisted of four meetings in addition to ongoing conversation leading up to the marriage.

Were you a part of a study or Bible group? If so, when was this into the relationship?

They did a home group together, two months into the relationship for about a month. They made a decision to continue after they were married. They also had a "Breakfast for Dinner" every Sunday night with their church friends. Everyone would bring $5 and chip in. Patrick was also a part of a friend group that met regularly and was leading a group of high school guys every Wednesday, while she met every Wednesday morning with her girlfriends for an hour to check in and talk about the relationship and life in general.

Did you discuss what religion would look like in your family (e.g., go to church weekly or more than weekly; involvement of church in daily life and finances; if children would go to Christian schools, etc.)?

Yes, church involvement for them would be significant. Patrick worked at the church (and still does). They had discussions about their involvement prior to their engagement. As a married couple, Kathryn now attends Patrick's staff meetings once a month and is more involved now than while they were dating.

When into the relationship did you discuss any obstacles or addictions that you needed to overcome (finances, anger, abuse, pornography, alcoholism, gambling, etc.)? Was the elimination of these addictions expected? How were these problems resolved?

Neither of them struggled with any addictions. She had to overcome her trust issues and learn not to be as guarded. They discussed how their past relationships were not healthy and had constant conversations about trust.

PART IV - DAILY LIFE

As independent as Kathryn carried herself and knowing how savvy this couple was, hearing that they spoke on the phone for half an hour daily kind of blew me away. I had imagined a string of text messages and snap chats as their daily correspondence. Another unpredicted finding was the amount of times they saw each other in a week and how active they were in each other's lives. I pictured him Facetiming her casually and squeezing her in his calendar maybe once a weekend. I imagined Kathryn was the same way. That's how it goes these days, right? Maybe not. The real deal was happening here, and I couldn't write down their notes fast enough. As a busy entrepreneur myself, it was enlightening to hear how much quality time they were able to have with one another even though she ran a successful photography business. My favorite tip from them was a very simple one: shared calendars. Genius! It took the guessing game out of when the other one was available or not and made the process a lot easier for those with a hectic schedule. A shared calendar also took the pressure off Patrick. Now he wouldn't ask for dates and feel shot down each time, because he could just look at Kathryn's calendar and see that she was scheduled to shoot a wedding that weekend. In return, she could see he had a staff meeting that night or an upcoming retreat. For me, that was such a useful tip during this interview.

For such a young couple, the boundaries they set were spot on. He seemed to have been mentored by someone well, making wise decisions setting boundaries including at work, with the opposite sex, and with Kathryn. It was clear he was truly guarding her heart, even though that meant not being physically as close to her as he wanted to be. Hearing his choices made me trust all his past choices, and I was proud of him, even though this was the first time I had met him. I was happy to hear all of the ways he sacrificed his comforts and waited to give his one and only his full self.

Did you speak daily early into the relationship? How long were your conversations at the beginning? When did this increase to a daily occurrence?

About one month into the relationship, they spoke about thirty minutes a day. This depended if they saw each other that day or not.

What type of communication was that generally more of—texting, phone conversations, FaceTime, in person, social media, etc.? How long typically were your conversations? How did your communication change as your relationship grew?

They had very light conversations at the beginning via phone and text. It was never through social media. They had more in-depth conversations face-to-face.

How many times a week did you see each other?

By the second month they saw each other four to five days a week.

When did you meet each other's core group of friends?

By month two, Patrick met Kathryn's two best friends. He might have met them earlier, it was around the holidays and things were crazy. She pretty much knew all of his friends before they started dating.

Did you discuss what type of movies to watch together? How did you handle it when one partner was uncomfortable with the content of the movie? What about TV shows, magazines, Internet activity?

It was understood between the both of them to not watch anything inappropriate or anything promoting nudity, etc. Patrick was very mindful of that and would turn the channel if it happened to come on. Mainly, he would not put himself in that situation and avoid it.

Did you go to each other's house? When watching movies or TV, did you lie down side by side, sit up right, or sit on separate couches?

He did not go into her house until the third or fourth date. They did not cuddle on the couch until around four months into the relationship. They would sit on the couch beside each other not even touching. They spooned on the couch after engagement but then had to stop as the temptation was too great.

Did you have other friends of the opposite sex while dating? Did you agree that as you became more intimately involved, those relationships would need to change? When into the relationship was this? How were those relationships changed?

Kathryn had a bunch of guy friends. She was aware that those relationships would need to change for Patrick's sake, and she quit being in touch with them unless in a group environment. She would never want to bring that into the relationship. If she sent a text to a guy, she would include a friend in a group text so it would never even make him doubt.

He did not have other relationships with other girls. He did not go to coffee, dinner, etc. with other women.

What were your boundaries with the opposite sex?

Boundaries were primarily just understood. He has a female assistant, and when they were in meetings, the doors were always open. He does not have lunch alone with his assistant or another woman, and there is always a third person in the car when driving somewhere.

Did you have a plan for times when one partner felt the other partner crossed the line with the opposite sex or made you feel uncomfortable? ex: You are at a friend's party, and your partner is talking to an attractive person of the opposite sex for a lengthy amount of time; an attractive coworker is talking to your partner longer than should be or spending too much time alone with them, etc.; your coworker is texting or Facebooking your partner.

They never put each other in those situations. She never doubted him, and vice versa.

PART V - SOCIAL MEDIA BOUNDARIES, EXPECTATIONS, AND ACCOUNTABILITY

What bewildered me the most was learning that Patrick would even ask Kathryn to look at his phone and read his messages aloud. I was almost confused by his answer as I have never experienced that. Most people these days seem to have such issues with looking at their phone, computer, or messages. Ding! I have learned from past experiences, if that is occurring, it's an enormous RED flag waving all over that person—no excuses. Having a completely open and honest relationship means doing the right thing off and online, in any form. This includes all social media, phones, and computers—everything. How are you supposed to get to know someone and think about a future with that person if you can't share the same phone or computer?

The need of complete transparency when using any social media platform is essential for a healthy, trustworthy foundation.

Whether sharing their social media messages, keeping one another in the loop, or even having group text messaging with the opposite sex, this couple was such a great example of allowing openness in that area. It was just plain awesome to hear and exciting for me to share with others. Personally, social media boundaries is my most favored topic. The need of complete transparency when using any social media platform is essential for a healthy, trustworthy foundation.

How did you keep each other accountable with social media while dating? Did this change after you were married?

Patrick keeps his posts primarily work based, and he works at the church. He did not post about their relationship until two to three months into it. They would post a picture of themselves at a baseball game for example. If a girl messaged him on Facebook, Kathryn always read it, and vice versa. It would usually be work related, however.

While dating, did you discuss how you would handle your social media? If so, when into the relationship was this? Were you free to check each other's phone logs, text messages, emails, Facebook messages, Internet activity, and social media interactions, etc.?

Patrick wasn't very active on Facebook, so they did not discuss it. Yes, they had the freedom to check each other's Facebook, phones, text messages, etc. They also started to share each other's Google calendars five months into the relationship and were able to schedule time with each other that way. They both had very busy calendars, so that allowed them to know what each other had going on.

Did you keep each other accountable on web browsing and viewing while dating? If you found something that made you feel uncomfortable, did you have open communication lines with your partner? What about after marriage?

They always pretty much knew what each other was looking up. Now if they are sitting on the couch together looking at their phones or computers they can openly ask what they are looking at. Most of the time Patrick is looking up sports-related stuff on his phone or computer, and Kathryn is looking up either clothes or dinner recipes. They have never really had a point where they had to question each other on what they were looking at, but they also had an open relationship that allowed them to ask each other at any time what is being searched.

Were either of you "friends" with previous girl/boyfriends on social media while dating? Did this affect the relationship? How was it handled?

In the past, once they broke up with someone, they had both removed that person from their social media channels.

After marriage:

Do you have one social media account or separate ones?

They have individual social media accounts.

Do you share and discuss when others contact you on social media platforms?

If they feel like they need to they will. If it is someone of the opposite sex contacting them that makes them feel weird then they say something. Other than that, they both have access to each other's accounts, so they have the freedom to ask or look if they need to. If something looks fishy on either account, they will address it. Most of the time it is a spam account commenting or someone neither of them knows. If you do not surround yourself or allow yourself to go there, it does not become an issue.

When someone messages that person through a social media channel, how is that handled?

If it is someone of the opposite sex, they show each other the message and read it so the other partner knows what is being said. They even tell each other what the response back is. It is an open communication of what is said back and forth from both parties.

Do you confront each other when you see a "like" or message that bothered you?

Yes, if they need to. But again, they trust each other. If they think it is inappropriate, then they say something and ask the other person to remove it or talk about why it bothers them.

Internet activity: How do you keep each other accountable for this? Do you monitor each other, have a program that monitors it, or have a friends that holds you accountable?

They are usually sitting beside each other and can view what the other person is looking at—he is usually looking at ESPN. He does not follow too many of his students and does not like social media. Sometimes a girl student will tag him in a picture for work. They have the freedom to check each other's accounts and both of their computers are logged into each other's accounts.

FINAL THOUGHTS FROM PATRICK AND KATHRYN

"There is not just one person for you. It is okay if you don't know if they are a fit on the first or second date. Don't stress about it and have a lot of fun."

Patrick and Kathryn were a classic example of a "don't judge a book by its cover" kind of couple. When I met Patrick, for some reason I was expecting different answers, though from Kathryn's past sharing of his character, I knew I was going to be interviewing a great guy. I was not anticipating, however, a man of his age having such strength and restraint in his current and past life choices. He genuinely impressed me. Kathryn equally impressed me, waiting for Patrick to arrive in her life. Even though she had heartbreak in her past, she healed and knew God would one day give her back those pieces and more than she could imagine. And after meeting him, she knew he was definitely worth the wait.

DISCUSSION QUESTIONS

- Your heart may have been broken in the past. You may have been let down and lied to. How are you going to let God do His work and help you through that pain to allow that next person to show you it can be overcome?
- Do you think that relationship devastated you because your boundaries were not set high enough to get to know that person well before you gave your heart away?
- Social media can make or break a relationship very fast these days. What parameters and understandings should you set with your current or future relationship?
- If your life is hectic and full, what methods or tools can you use to schedule quality time together and communicate effectively?

JONATHAN AND OLIVIA: [LONG-DISTANCE PURSUIT]

MEET JONATHAN AND OLIVIA:

AGES WHEN MARRIED:

Him: 32; Her: 24

LENGTH DATED:

10 months

LENGTH ENGAGED:

12 months

HOW LONG MARRIED NOW:

1.5 years

HOW THEY MET:

Olivia and Jonathan met at a mutual friend's wedding in Mexico but both resided in Florida. He asked her to dance at the wedding, and they spent time together talking. They knew of each other their whole lives but never crossed paths. Both lived nearby, knew each other's families, and went to the same neighborhood pool. He was a coach for her competitor's swim team.

Over the past couple of years, I have had the privilege to observe the behaviors and interactions between Olivia and Jonathan every Tuesday night. That is because that's the night our small group meets every week for a couple of hours. I admit when I first met this couple, I thought they were too active and athletic in nature for me to have that much in common with them. Mind you, I'm also an active person, but I feel they are on a different level. Olivia was a former star swimmer and is still very athletic; Jonathan was an adventurer seeker and would jump off just about *anything* that seemed like a challenge. My Pilates and walks around the neighborhood just didn't seem to quite match up to their level of thrill seeking and competitive natures. But after a couple of months of slowly getting to know them, my first impressions turned around completely. This amazing, smart-as-a-whip, athletic woman had a soft feminine side that slowly started to come out of her each time I saw her. She opened up a little bit at a time to the group, and I was one of the few people who experienced her emotional side. Being an engineer by profession and out in the field, Olivia was generally in male-dominated groups, which required her to keep her true feminine feelings hidden while on duty. Jonathan was actually in the health care industry, so it surprised me to witness this burly, iron-type man tap into his emotional, caring side.

After getting to know Olivia and Jonathan on a deeper level, I was so intrigued by them and how they connected to one another that I knew they were the perfect fit for the book. Jonathan was always attentive to Olivia, completely engaged while she spoke and shared with our group. He would unconsciously caress her when the time was needed, wipe away her tears as they came, and I will never forget the moment he stepped in to finish her difficult story when she could not. That was the moment I knew I wanted to know more about them, what brought them together, and how to seek for myself what they had.

What attracted you to this person in the beginning?

Olivia's smile, jovial spirit, and beauty initially attracted Jonathan. Later on it was her heart for God. He was very honest, genuine, low key, and mellow—that attracted her. He was able to speak freely without preconceived notions. She listened to him give a speech on love at the wedding and that also attracted her. She liked that he wanted to talk without making her feel like he wanted anything other than just good company. She felt that they connected through conversation and they shared similar morals.

What characteristics were you looking for in your future partner?

Jonathan says: Someone who had a heart for God and who was adventurous is what I was looking for. I could see that in Olivia by the way she talked about the activities she chose to do. She told me she was going to do a service trip for indigent communities in Peru, to help build and install wind turbines.

Olivia says: For me, it was Jonathan's heart for God. I wanted a relationship right with God, and Jonathan's faith was strong. His intelligence was also what I was seeking. It was evident God was first in his life, not getting a girl.

Did he automatically lead from the start of contact? What did that look like? (woman's perspective)

The same night he met her, he went on top of the hotel roof to talk to God. It was for prayer and thanksgiving. He prayed he was thankful to have met a woman like her.

Jonathan led Olivia from the start. He initially came up to her at the wedding. He also went on telling his story of when he found a rock in the shape of a heart on a beach a year prior to meeting her. He felt God was saying to him, like in Ezekiel 36:26, there was hope and not to be bitter, to start new and pure.

He shared his intentions with her on their second date. It was important for her to know his past experiences and what his expectations were. He threw the rock into the ocean. It symbolized starting new, so throwing it in the ocean was important.

Olivia agreed that Jonathan had led from the start. After the wedding, he asked her to go to a water park. On the bus, she walked in front of everyone from the wedding party to the back of the bus and let him know she would go with him to the water park. That was her way of showing she was interested. They went to the water park at 7am the morning before her flight at 12pm. When they got back from Mexico, he messaged her the next day on Facebook. He knew she was leaving for Peru very soon after that, followed by heading to Germany for another two weeks and then moving to New York! He wanted to see her before she left. Turns out, he changed his flight to come back home earlier in hopes of seeing her. He didn't tell her that he changed his flight. They ended up having two dates before she left for two weeks in Peru.

What form of communication had been your primary one? Did you talk about if you prefer to text, see each other, or talk on the phone?

They used the phone as their primary communication. At the beginning, they talked for about an hour once a week.

When into the relationship did you discuss your intentions and expectations for the relationship? Who brought it up?

On the second date Jonathan shared his intentions and expectations. When Olivia came back from Peru, he gave her a book, *Choosing God's Best* by Dr. Don Raunikar.

When do you think you grew close to her? To him?

For Jonathan, it was around Thanksgiving, about six months into the relationship, when he really began to feel close to Olivia. They had a kayaking date. It was the first time he was annoyed with her because she was bumping into everything, and she was on the rowing team! Her version of the story is that she was so good at rowing, and he was doing it all wrong! This is an ongoing joke with them, so each must have not been trying to show off for the other's sake. Afterwards they went to the beach and had a serious talk.

When New Year's came around, they spent time together, and he was just grateful for her company. They went out dancing and had fun. The combination of that time spent together and liking her family was what drew him close to her.

For Olivia, it was both after they went kayaking and on New Year's, which was seven months into the relationship. After they went kayaking and had that very deep conversation, she opened up as well. After that day they talked more frequently. She liked how he was just enjoying the friendship and was very patient and humble. She saw the way he treated his mom and young cousins, and that New Year's Day he made her lobster bisque from scratch. She told him she was ready to be with him now.

When did you first say *I love you*? Did you have the intention at that point for marriage?

Jonathan told Olivia that he loved her on Valentine's Day. Yes, he had the intention of marriage at that point. It was eight months into the relationship. She told him she loved him at that same time.

At what point in the relationship did you "know" you desired each other as your marriage partner? What was it that made you know? Was it a feeling or was something done?

For Jonathan it was after their conversation on the beach. He saw her true motives with her faith and that God came first. Seeing her with her family—she fit in perfectly with his family also—it was meant to be.

For Olivia it was a little later—one day before he proposed. She almost broke up with him two days before he proposed, but God opened her heart that day, and she knew. She was clear then with herself that she was never breaking up with anyone again. Opening up his past accelerated her feelings as well as watching him interact with family and friends.

Did you discuss what love language you responded to? If so, when did you start acting upon that? Was this done before, during, or after the engagement?

Yes, after they got engaged they took *The Five Love Languages* test that helped them figure out what their love languages were. They had the same love language: physical touch. However, they were not able to use their primary love language in dating, so that was difficult. It works great in marriage now.

Do you feel waiting for sexual intimacy sped up the dating process?

Absolutely on his end. Jonathan pointed out it forces you to be more intentional about dating. Olivia said waiting probably sped up the dating process for her as well.

How hard was it to maintain the commitment before sexual intimacy?

It was something he said you have to talk about and think about before the relationship. You have to remember the rule and why. It was very hard for her. It was almost a habit that you develop, and it made it harder at the beginning because she was used to relationships being a certain way. Knowing his intentions made a difference. When they became engaged, it was like hitting a reset button for her because there was a finish line. She mentioned it takes both people to be 100% committed to this. It did not work for her in previous relationships when only one person desired to wait for sexual intimacy.

Did you discuss your sexual past or past partners, if any? When did you start to discuss this?

Yes, they discussed their past on the beach day in November (six months into the relationship). Early on, it was a crucial step made explicit on the beach on why they were waiting. He wanted her to be in that vision. For her, she knew then that he had those values.

PART II - BOUNDARIES AND ACCOUNTABILITY

One night after small group, Jonathan told me about the book, *Choosing God's Best,* he gave Olivia. He thought it would help me in my search. He truly stunned me that *he* was the one that gave her that book. I have not only never known a guy who did that, I have never heard of one doing that either. Even though I was surrounded by Christian men in my church, that mystified me. In my past experiences, it was always me making and setting boundaries, however minimal those were. Hearing how Jonathan took the reins from the initial start and took leadership in the progression of the relationship was exciting for me to learn about, especially in these days of hurried happiness. I purchased the book that night.

Describe your first date:

Their first date was at a water park in Mexico early in the morning before her flight back to Florida. They both shared a love for swimming and exercise so it was a good first date to get to know each other's interests.

Did you establish boundaries from the get go? Who led that conversation?

The boundary of waiting until marriage to be physically intimate was set very early on. They established boundaries together but really did not talk about it much. He lived at his mom's house in Florida, and she lived in New York but had a roommate. He stayed at her place in New York and slept in her same bed. She was intentional on what she wore to bed. He moved to New York in July, and they were engaged then. However, he still got his own place, even though it was very expensive.

What boundaries did you create? Did you have the same boundaries?

They set the boundaries not to live with each other and not to have sex prior to marriage.

How did you hold each other accountable to those boundaries?

They kept each other accountable; it takes both people to keep each other accountable. They both set boundaries to not live together before they were married, and they also agreed to do premarital counseling. Sometimes she would stay at her friend's house and not sleep in his bed. He was bitter about that because he knew he could trust himself, and he wanted to get close. Now looking back, he says he respects her more for doing that.

When did you start holding hands? What date was your first kiss?

They held hands at Thanksgiving (three months into the relationship), and their first kiss was on their second date. After their first kiss there was a long pause until Christmas. He was not ready for it, it was premature.

How did you control your sexual desires for each other? Did you discuss the difficulty of controlling your desire for each other?

Yes, they discussed that it was difficult. When he would express that to her, she found it helpful to take practical steps back, including staying at a friend's house when visiting out of town. Even if this made him mad, it was better for them. Not seeing each other on a regular basis helped. They got to know each other through their phone calls. For around three months they would not see each other, and then they would be together for a couple of days at a time.

Time limits are very important as a boundary so that being with that person doesn't turn into an obsession. It forces you not to rely on that person as your only source of happiness.

Time limits are very important as a boundary so that being with that person doesn't turn into an obsession. It forces you not to rely on that person as your only source of happiness.

Was this a local or long-distance relationship? Can you offer advice on long-distance relationships (if so, did you stay at each other's place, how often do you see each other, should the man visit the woman more or equal, etc.)?

Yes, this was a long-distance relationship. Their advice is to not live together and to stay at a friend's house if possible while dating. They also suggest making an extra effort to meet each other's families and not to spend the holidays together until you feel ready.

Did you ever spend the night at each other's house? Was this in the same bed? Were there other people in the house at the time? What was the situation?

Yes, there were times when he went to visit her in New York that they stayed the night together in the same bed. She had a roommate at that time as well.

Did you mainly do daytime dates? Did you do more group or one-on-one dating? Any overnight trips?

Dates were mainly daytime and one-on-one. They included a lot of outdoor activities including kayaking, fishing, and skiing. He would also come over and eat with her family. They had their first overnight trip in February (when they had been dating eight months) and stayed in the same room together.

At what point did you have a relationship and open discussions with his family, including seeing you involved as a part of the future family unit?

Her father passed away so he was unable to ask for his blessing. He never discussed marriage with her mother, but they had dinners with both families often. They knew each other's families very well.

Did you have a close person in your life that held you accountable, truly had your best interest in mind, and gave you advice?

Not until they were engaged. After engagement, they had a premarital counselor to hold them accountable and give advice.

PART III - A CHRIST-CENTERED RELATIONSHIP

It took me back a bit how Jonathan and Olivia did not have a particularly large involvement of church during their time of dating. Surely, I thought, they would be at church every Wednesday night and passing out meals on the weekends. During their marriage now, they are very devoted to Christ and have such a relentless spiritual bond. Having a strong spiritual foundation was critical to one another when they met, but they were more independent in their worship during their dating and engagement. Their relationship with Christ grew with each other after they were married and shared that marriage covenant.

The first time you shared a meal; did he offer to bless the meal?

Yes, he blessed the meal the first time and thereafter.

Were you raised with the same religious backgrounds and values?

Yes.

Did you come from the same faith or denomination?

Both grew up Catholic and had similar lifestyles. In high school, she started to become non-denominational. He became non-denominational after they were married.

Did you attend the same church when you met? If not, whose church did you start attending, and when did you start attending together?

Only after marriage did they attend the same church. Now they are non-denominational. They were very conflicted because his family are devout Catholics.

When did you start praying together?

Early, right at the beginning.

Did you serve together while you were dating? Were they the same roles, e.g., both on the coffee team or one serving in children's ministry and other serving as a greeter, etc.?

Once they served at a soup kitchen at Christmas time. He initiated that. They were not able to serve together regularly because of long-distance.

Did you establish a mentor relationship with other strong Christian married couples while dating?

Not until premarital counseling, but they wish they'd had mentors.

Did you do any type of workbook or study together? If so, when was this into the relationship? Did you think this was valuable?

They used the book he gave her, *Choosing God's Best* by Dr. Don Raunkiar. He gave her this book very early, right at the beginning. It was valuable to them. Sharing the book with her before they started dating set the foundation of the relationship. After their engagement, they did a workbook called *The Meaning of Marriage* by Timothy and Kathy Keller.

Did you participate in premarital counseling after engagement?

Yes, they had six sessions with another couple.

Were you a part of a study or Bible group? If so, when was this into the relationship?

Neither of them were in a study or group while dating; they were only in a community group style.

Were you a part of a weekly community group? If so, when was this into the relationship?

They both were in a coed community group in their respective churches. He started to go with her after the engagement. After marriage, they joined a church and community group together.

Did you discuss what religion would look like in your family, e.g., go to church weekly or more than weekly; involvement of church in daily life and finances; if children would have Christian schooling, etc.?

They discussed which church they would go to and tithing when they were engaged. They did not discuss children at that point. Yes, they discussed going weekly to church.

When into the relationship did you discuss any obstacles or addictions that you needed to overcome (finances, anger, abuse, pornography, alcoholism, gambling, etc.)? Was the elimination of these addictions expected? How were these problems resolved?

Jonathan had past issues with finances and pornography and disclosed these early in the relationship, on the kayaking day, that it was in his past. Olivia loved that he brought up those issues on his own. By telling her, he owned it and held himself accountable. Yes, the elimination of these were expected. He had already overcome his addiction to pornography and was actively working to improve his finances by putting into practice techniques learned in a biblical financial class. He resolved these by selling some of his stuff and took steps to prevent failing. He sold luxury items he owned to pay off credit card debt and committed to living a humble lifestyle and eliminating debt.

Diving deeper into Jonathan's struggle with pornography, I was grateful for his willingness to share his journey to overcome his struggle and how he currently manages it. Hopefully his story will be helpful for others needing to overcome this powerful addiction:

Jonathan had a personal struggle with the sin of lusting from the time he was a young boy until he reached adulthood. As early as elementary school, he saw his first nude magazine. Jonathan remembered the feelings it elicited—intense curiosity and attraction and feelings of guilt—yet he could not explain why he was embarrassed or why he had to hide the magazine. The lusting, coupled with a habit of masturbation, elicited arousal and brief moments of pleasure but came with longer periods of remorse and extreme dissatisfaction with himself. As he moved into teenage years, the problem became worse with easy access to pornographic material on the Internet.

It wasn't until college when he joined a church group and began a relationship with the Lord that he felt he needed to remove these sinful activities from his life.

In the short term, it was helpful to download a program to his computer to block pornographic websites. However, similar to putting a lock on your fridge to stop binging on ice cream, this solution was short lived, since he could lust in a myriad of other ways.

It became clear to Jonathan that his inability to conquer his lustful desires was due to spiritual weakness, not just a physical one. So, he signed up for retreats offered by his church. He prayed fervently and saw improvements. He was fortunate to meet a brother-in-Christ on a church retreat, and they became good friends. He soon felt that he needed to confess his sin to someone in order to begin the process of cutting the sin from his life. They confessed their struggles to one another and were able to encourage each other in abolishing the habit of self-serving behaviors. Having someone who he could talk to openly about this sin, and who would give him advice rooted in Scripture, was a big step forward, although this alone was not enough to eradicate the sin: after years of engaging in a behavior and mindset, it's extremely difficult to make a lasting change. Jonathan realized that he needed to move in small steps, and it was going to be a process of seeking the Lord rather than relying on sheer willpower to abstain. He needed to completely change his heart and mind. Instead of simply attempting to stop sinning, he needed to figure out what to replace the sin with. In essence, he needed to learn to live like a true disciple of Christ.

His church routinely asked for volunteers to serve at a soup kitchen run by Catholic nuns, so he began to volunteer there. By serving the homeless, the marginalized, and the outcasts of society as Jesus did, his perspective began to change. Instead of serving his own interests and desires, he learned to put others before himself.

Jonathan still found himself sinning, though it was with much less frequency than before. The stronghold that the sin had over his life was weakening. He despised the sin but was also frustrated that it was taking so long to overcome it, and he felt powerless each time he fell back into sin. It was a vulnerable period because his failures lead to discouragement and doubt about whether he would truly change. He knew that at the root of the issue, he still needed to surrender to God and stop resisting His sovereignty over all aspects of Jonathan's life, including relationships and sexuality.

In the process of learning to live for Christ, Jonathan began to see the beauty and meaning of marriage and God's plan for sexuality. He made a decision to allow God to take control of his relationships after he read *Choosing God's Best* that highlighted the importance of purity and courting a woman for marriage rather than dating her.

When he met the woman who would become his wife, he knew that he wanted to honor her and love her in the way God intended. The only way to do that was to confess his sins to her, share with her his struggles, and live as a believer and follower of Christ. Very early in their courtship, Jonathan shared his past sin with her, knowing that she might no longer want to see him. But he felt that if they were going to pursue a serious relationship, she deserved to know all about him. By confessing to her, he entrusted the relationship completely to God. He experienced overwhelming mercy and joy when she affirmed the Apostle Paul's message to the Corinthians: "Therefore, if anyone is in Christ, he is a new creation." Hearing those words and experiencing God's compassion changed his heart forever and allowed him to live in freedom from the bondage that had paralyzed him for so long.

His wife later told him that this was a significant day in their relationship because it showed her that seeking God's will was more important to him than seeking her approval. By His grace, they now share a beautiful marriage centered on Christ. His selfish desires and sinful behaviors have given way to a desire to lead a righteous life—one that is under the authority of Christ and one that brings true happiness, meaning, and joy.

PART IV - DAILY LIFE

Jonathan and Olivia demonstrated that if you want a relationship to work, given any life situations, you can make it work with effort and a Christ-centered focus. They beat the odds of living in different cities, one partner needing more time to fully commit and constantly on the move. Knowing how involved they are in each other's lives now, it was hard to believe they used to talk on the phone only a couple of nights a week and see each other with even a month or two in between. If a couple can make it through meeting at a wedding in Mexico, staying abroad twice directly after meeting one another, and moving to a complete other city, it showed me a man will not allow a circumstance to stop his pursuit. Jonathan followed his heart and trusted God to help him. He was going to prove to Olivia that he would wait and follow her, wherever and however long it took.

Did you speak daily early into the relationship? How long were your conversations at the beginning? When did this increase to a daily occurrence?

Daily speaking was not needed every day because they trusted each other. At the beginning, conversations were about an hour in length, and after engagement they saw each other on a daily basis.

What type of communication was that generally more of—texting, phone conversations, FaceTime, in person, social media, etc.? How long typically were your conversations? How did your communication change as your relationship grew?

Jonathan and Olivia mainly had phone conversations, about one to two times a week for about an hour per call for a while and then transitioned to every other day. The conversations were more in-depth, longer ones. They saw each other once every three months for seven days until they were engaged. Then he moved to New York for her, and they saw each other every day.

How many times a week did you see each other?

After he moved to New York, they saw each other almost every day for one month. Then she was sent out of town on a work assignment for six months.

When did you meet each other's core group of friends?

He met her best friend on the day he proposed. He wanted her to be surrounded by her family and best friend. Jonathan didn't meet Olivia's other friends until after he proposed. During their first month of dating, they went on some group dates to meet each other's friends.

Did you discuss what type of movies to watch together? How did you handle it when one partner was uncomfortable with the content of the movie? What about TV shows, magazines, Internet activity?

Yes, they had that conversation about certain types of movies being harmful, especially those sexual in nature for men struggling with pornography. She respected his reasons for not seeing certain types of movies and vice versa.

Did you go to each other's house? When watching movies or TV, did you lie down side by side, sit up right, or sit on separate couches?

They went to each other's house but were never alone and watched movies lying side by side. They did lie down on the couch beside each other when watching movies, etc. While engaged they spent time alone at each other's house.

Did you have other friends of the opposite sex while dating? Did you agree that as you became more intimately involved, those relationships would need to change? How did you handle that? When into the relationship was this? How were those relationships changed?

Yes, she had a male roommate and eventually had that roommate move out as the relationship progressed. On his end, he had a long-time friend from his community group who was a female. Jonathan and his friend would occasionally go to the movies together, and he would pick her up. He considered her like a sister. After their engagement, that relationship changed, and he no longer had one-on-one time with her.

What were your boundaries with the opposite sex?

She works in a male-dominated industry in which most of her coworkers are men, so boundaries had to be established. The field that she is in requires her to have frequent communication with the opposite sex, so trust had to be established. Clear boundaries were set with the other men, including not meeting one-on-one with another male in a hotel room. Most interactions are in groups. If she has to meet one-on-one with a male coworker, it is always in the lobby or a public place.

Did you establish to set an open and safe conversation when one partner felt the other partner crossed the line with the opposite sex or made them feel uncomfortable?

Yes.

PART V - SOCIAL MEDIA BOUNDARIES, EXPECTATIONS, AND ACCOUNTABILITY

During the interview, I asked about what accounts Jonathan was following on Instagram, and it came up that he followed a lot of fishing-related accounts. Olivia mentioned that sometimes a girl can pop up in a bathing suit and specifically mentioned one person Jonathan was following, which happened to be a female fisherwoman. She looked through his pictures while they were sitting on the couch beside each other, and she did not care for some of them, as this particular lady he was following had some slightly provocative pictures. I looked at them and agreed. Jonathan asked her if she wanted him to stop following the woman, and she said yes. It was not a big deal, he agreed and instantly unfollowed her. Overall, it took a few minutes of conversation and an action step, and then it was over with both parties understanding each other.

Even though that was a small moment in the grand scheme of things, it was a large moment for *me*. I was able to view how social media in an instant can drive a wedge between a couple if they let it. If Jonathan had for one split second fought against the notion of unfollowing that woman, it could have knocked down Olivia's confidence and trust in seconds. I realized that those small decisions you make as a couple have a tremendous impact overall. Having a complete understanding of what is important to the other partner and respecting each other is essential to building and sustaining trust in a relationship.

That was a great moment.

How did you keep each other accountable with social media while dating? Did this change after you were married?

Prior to their marriage, they talked about social media boundaries and had up front communication. For example, Jonathan came to Olivia one day and said that he had unfriended someone that day because she had been posting lots of bikini pictures. He said he did not want to see that and wanted to respect Olivia. He did this without her even knowing about the girl posting those pictures, which built trust. After marriage, they still have open communication with each other. A part of that includes neither spouse being connected to past relationships. They are open with each other and often look at Facebook and other social media platforms together.

> Having a complete understanding of what is important to the other partner and respecting each other is essential to building and sustaining trust in a relationship.

Did you discuss how you would handle your social media interactions and accounts? During courtship and engagements, were you free to check each other's phone logs, text messages, emails, Facebook messages, Internet activity, and social media interactions, etc.?

They agreed to remove pictures from Facebook that included people they had previously been involved with. They were fully trusting of each other's activities so there was no need to monitor each other's accounts.

Did you keep each other accountable on web browsing and viewing while dating? If you found something that made you feel uncomfortable, did you have open communication lines with your partner? What about after marriage?

Olivia occasionally checked in with Jonathan to see if he was watching pornography. He wasn't, so it was not an issue.

Were either of you "friends" with previous girlfriends or boyfriends on social media while dating? Did this affect the relationship? How was it handled?

They removed pictures from their social media and unfriended people we'd been involved with in the past.

After marriage:

Do you have one social media account or separate ones?

They each have an individual account.

Do you share and discuss when others contact you on social media platforms?

They let each other know when someone messages them or anything they need to let the other partner know about.

When someone messages that person through a social media channel, how is that handled?

They talk to each other about that; everything is transparent and open.

Do you confront each other when you see a "like" or message that bothers you?

They have an open dialogue and will let each other know if anything bothers them.

Internet activity: How do you keep each other accountable for this? Do you monitor each other, have a program that monitors it, or have a friend that hold you accountable?

They have each other's passwords on all emails, social media accounts, or otherwise. They each have full permission to look at the other's phone, texts, any messages, etc.

FINAL THOUGHTS FROM JONATHAN AND OLIVIA

"Relationships can be especially confusing and difficult to navigate. Sometimes our own emotions betray us: infatuation can be mistaken with love, and feelings can be very deceiving. It is easy to confuse the feeling of lust, which is selfish, for love, which is unselfish. It is important that we recognize what real love looks like so that we pursue the right thing. In the Bible we learn that love is not merely a feeling. Love is putting the other before you. Love is sacrificial, it's unselfish, it's generous, abundant, and it flows from God. Everything good comes from God. Love isn't something we have to search for—it's something we have to practice!"

It is easy to confuse the feeling of lust, which is selfish, for love, which is unselfish. It is important that we recognize what real love looks like so that we pursue the right thing.

"One of the fruits of trusting God with our relationships is that He allows us to see clearly and make the right decisions. If we are in a relationship that is not godly, we must not be afraid to end it. We have a tendency to ignore or make excuses for why our inner voice is wrong, but prolonging the wrong relationship only keeps you from being with the person that God wants for you. Seek the Lord first, abandon your will, and fully surrender to Him. Learn to be content and show love to others. When you live the gospel adventurously you will attract the right people, those that also put God first, and then you can build a foundation of true love together as He intended."

Jonathan and Olivia exemplified to me what waiting and sacrifice really looked like. Jonathan wanted to move a lot more quickly than Olivia did, but he patiently waited for her to catch up. He let God lead the way to her heart, and it paid off. Olivia also let God lead the way, allowing time for her to trust Jonathan and know that he would lead and pursue her. It makes sense knowing the thrill seeker Jonathan is. Olivia was his adventure—and he finally found her.

DISCUSSION QUESTIONS

- Are you willing to sacrifice time and distance for a long-distance relationship? What time frame does that look like for you?
- Would you be open to moving for that person?
- What boundaries will you set if in a long-distance relationship? Where will you stay? How much time will you spend together?
- If you discover your partner has past addictions, how will you deal with it? Do you expect those addictions to be resolved before continuing the relationship, or are you willing to be there for that person during that time?

COLIN AND ELIZA: [MODERN MIX]

MEET COLIN AND ELIZA:

AGES WHEN MARRIED:

Him: 29; Her: 26

DIFFERENCE IN AGES:

3 years

LENGTH DATED:

6 months

LENGTH ENGAGED:

6 months

HOW LONG MARRIED NOW:

7 years

LENGTH OF FIRST MARRIAGE:

Prior to meeting Eliza, Colin had been married for six years. Four of those years he was married, and two of those years he was separated. This is Eliza's first marriage.

ANY CHILDREN PRIOR TO MARRIAGE:

He had a three-year-old and a five-year-old daughter. Since their marriage, they now have a child of their own.

HOW THEY MET:

They met through their dentist. She had just broken up with her unfaithful fiancé and was upset when she saw her dentist. He asked her what type of man she was looking for and said he was going to intentionally find her someone. He asked around and thought one of his male clients would be a good fit, and so he connected the two.

A few years ago at a Bible study, I met this cute, petite blonde who loved wearing large silver hoops. The darnedest, most frank, honest words and thoughts would come out of this gal. I loved it! Sometimes you think of Bible study, especially a women's study, as being particularly, well . . . stuffy. Not this one. This little bundle of light came in and shared whatever was on her mind. It was what I needed. She didn't hide her past or her feelings, opening up and letting a group of ladies get to know her intimately. I was grateful for those studies and always interested when it was her turn to speak.

During this time, she was also dating her now-husband Colin. Even though I was there through their dating process and attended their wedding, this interview is what truly uncovered how much more was going on behind the scenes than I realized. It was quite fun to reminisce and hear the scoop on all the details.

What attracted you to this person in the beginning?

Colin was at a physical therapy session and decided to quickly look Eliza up on Myspace after their mutual dentist connected them. He thought she was cute, so he texted her and misspelled her name. She immediately corrected his text with the correct

He shared his salvation testimony very quickly with her; she knew they were pursuing the same thing.

spelling of her name. He thought she was a bit sassy when she did that and liked it. He let her know he would call her later. They talked all night, and the next day he had to see her in person, so he drove to her work. Physically, she was everything he wanted. They talked for hours about everything before they even met.

The fact that Colin loved God attracted Eliza. He was a strong Christian, which was his top priority. He was the one who asked about her involvement in her church and also how she served. He shared his salvation testimony very quickly with her; she knew they were pursuing the same thing.

What characteristics were you looking for in your future partner?

He was seeking a godly woman. He saw in his church a lot of Christian couples, and Colin knew he wanted what those couples had. He wanted to share that same connection and to lead in that way. He could have looked past the physical, but it was a bonus. She was equally looking for a godly man.

Did he automatically lead from the start of contact? What did that look like? (woman's perspective)

She is more of a type-A personality, while Colin is more on the passive side. He struggled with *not* taking the lead. However, he led directly from the start and also led them in going to church.

What form of communication had been your primary one? Did you talk about if you prefer to text, see each other, or talk on the phone?

They saw each other every day in person. They also texted, spoke on the phone, and wrote emails to each other.

When into the relationship did you discuss your intentions and expectations for the relationship? Who brought it up?

Within two weeks of meeting each other, they discussed intentions and expectations, and he led that conversation.

When do you think you grew close to her? To him?

There was not a single moment Colin can pinpoint. They were both constantly moving in the direction of each other. She met his ex-wife around five to six months into the relationship. It was hard for her meeting his ex-wife because she was upset that he had already been married. He saw it as an opportunity to bring Christ into his ex-wife's life, who had not been a believer. Eliza was jealous of their phone calls. Now that they're married, Eliza is the only one who talks to the ex-wife and does all of the scheduling with her. She uses her strength in planning.

For Eliza, it was by the second week when they started to see each other every day. She met the kids one month into the relationship. The children were hard for her; they were just a different personality than she was used to. She would go over to Colin's house and help put them to bed, and later Colin and Eliza would watch a movie.

When did you first say I love you? Did you have the intention at that point for marriage?

Since she had experienced a bad past relationship, Eliza wanted to make sure they still felt that passionate about each other.

They said they loved each other within two weeks and wanted to marry each other. Eliza was everything Colin wanted. Two to three months into the relationship, he started to talk to his community leader about how long he should date before asking Eliza to marry him. Colin's leader said he already knew what he wanted. He always wanted to be with her. They saw each other every day. Typically, he gets really excited about things and then he's had enough, but with her he never *not* wanted to be with her.

She felt the same way but told him she wanted to wait and see if he felt the same way about her in six months. Since she had experienced a bad past relationship, Eliza wanted to make sure they still felt that passionate about each other.

At what point in the relationship did you "know" you desired each other as your marriage partner? What was it that made you know? Was it a feeling or was something done?

Colin was the whole package to her: godliness, looks, morals. It was the yin and yang of everyday life. Eliza's weaknesses were Colin's strengths and vice versa. However, she wanted to make sure she was not being immature about it and wanted to reassure the relationship with time.

He liked how she enjoyed every moment in life. It was a balance of personality for him.

Did you discuss what love language you responded to? When did you start acting upon that? Was this done before, during, or after the engagement?

Both of their love languages were personal touch. He held her hands or touched her back, and they put their arms around each other.

Do you feel waiting for sexual intimacy sped up the dating process?

Yes, because they were not having sex.

How hard was it to maintain the commitment before sexual intimacy?

They would both stop when they got too physical. He would have had so much guilt and shame if he had ever taken it too far. She pointed out that being engaged does not mean you are getting married. She was engaged to another man prior to meeting him, and he was unfaithful to her during that engagement. Now that she looks back, her ex-fiancé was always pushing her to have sex, and she is thankful she waited to give that gift to her husband.

Now that she looks back, her ex-fiancé was always pushing her to have sex, and she is thankful she waited to give that gift to her husband.

It was very hard for them. There was a time at the beach they shared the same room, and it was very difficult for them to control their intimacy.

Did you discuss your sexual past or past partners, if any? When did you start to discuss this?

Because they committed themselves to each other early on, it was one of their first conversations within their first week. She let him know in the first week that she was a virgin, and he told her he was a re-born virgin. He shared his salvation story with her within their first conversations, including his sexual past.

PART II - BOUNDARIES AND ACCOUNTABILITY

Sharing the details of Colin and Eliza's initial date for the first time brought massive smiles to their faces. This couple always had one thing they blatantly shared—intense attraction. For lack of a better description, they were always hot for one another. If *this* couple can make it through the boundary section on lust and save sexual intimacy until marriage, any couple can. She was everything he desired, and he was hers. During the interview, the deep rapture they found in one another was still there; it had never left. In fact, it was more so, and it was apparent their marriage drew them into a sharper and stronger bond with each other.

Describe your first date:

It was about a week after they first spoke that they had their first date. He picked her up at her sister's house, and they went to a Brazilian restaurant. This was a sweet touch since she grew up in Brazil, so he catered to what she would like to eat. After the restaurant they went back to his place where he set up two tents in the backyard. He was really into camping at the time. They slept in their own individual tents that night, even though it was raining and her tent was leaking. The next morning, he drove her home.

Did you establish boundaries from the get go? Who led that conversation?

They had boundary conversations constantly. Boundaries were understood, but they were constantly readjusting as there was always sexual tension.

What boundaries did you create? Did you have the same boundaries?

She went home by 10pm every night and always stayed out of his bedroom. Keeping that routine of being gone by a decent time kept it understood. He was taking sleeping medication at the time so they would talk all the way home, which was about fifteen minutes away. On the first big night they talked there was no kissing. The first night they hung out at his house, he kissed her. That continued on for weeks. Then it got more intense. Every time they would go too far, they would re-evaluate and police themselves. Their advice for other couples is to keep the bedroom off limits.

How did you hold each other accountable to those boundaries?

Living with her sister held her accountable. That is key.

When did you start holding hands? What date was your first kiss?

Their first kiss was before their official date, and they started holding hands right away, but they do not remember an exact moment.

How did you control your sexual desires for each other? Did you discuss the difficulty of controlling your desire for each other?

He would sit on a separate couch from her if things got too hot and heavy, or she would leave. They talked a lot about this problem and how to avoid it.

Was this a local or long-distance relationship? Can you offer advice on long-distance relationships?

This was a local relationship. Advice for other couples is to stay with a friend while dating long-distance and to keep the bedroom off limits.

Did you ever spend the night at each other's house? Was this in the same bed? Were there other people in the house at the time? What was the situation?

No.

Did you mainly do daytime dates? Did you do more group or one-on-one dating? Any overnight trips?

They were mainly all evening dates because they both worked. Most dates were more one-on-one and hanging out with each other. She would help him do laundry, clean the house, organize his bills. He mentioned he thought, "I need to put a ring on her finger!" They were basically hanging out and doing activities like they were married but without the sex. He let her know this was his life; he had kids. He did not have a lot of money to go on fancy dates. Money was an issue, so they would cook together.

At what point did you have a relationship and open discussions with his family, including seeing you involved as a part of the future family unit?

He told his parents within two weeks, and they met her a month later. They loved her, and there was no tension from his family. Her family was against it because he was divorced. Her family lived out of the country. They both had counseling from their preacher and small group leader on that matter.

PART III - A CHRIST-CENTERED RELATIONSHIP

Finding out how each couple brought Christ into their relationship at different paces was one of the prized bits of information I gathered during the interviews. Knowing Eliza through Bible studies, I assumed she and Colin would have had these profound prayers and study sessions together. It was the exact opposite. They prayed lightly with one another as they dated, but remained closer to Christ individually. Eliza and Colin attended church and served together, but ultimately they waited until marriage to be completely spiritually united.

The first time you shared a meal; did he offer to bless the meal?

Yes, he did.

Were you raised with the same religious backgrounds and values?

They were both raised in Christian homes; hers was very strict.

Did you come from the same faith or denomination?

She was raised in a very conservative Independent Baptist home, and he grew up non-denominational. When they met they were both in the same spiritual place.

Did you attend the same church when you met? If not, whose church did you start attending, and when did you start attending together?

He took her to his church the second Sunday they met. He did not like her church, and she loved his church. (He had been very concerned that she wouldn't like his church.) For about a month, she was going to both her and his church. After that she switched over to his church and went every Sunday, getting involved in a lot of serving opportunities and Bible study two to three days a week.

When did you start praying together?

They prayed before meals and with his kids. They did not really start praying together until they got married.

Did you serve together while you were dating? Were they the same roles?

They both served in the children's ministry, but in different positions. He did the sound part and she was a coach, so they were in the same place doing different things.

Did you establish a mentor relationship with other strong Christian married couples while dating?

Yes, they had premarital counselors while they were engaged.

Did you do any type of workbook or study together? If so, when was this into the relationship? Did you think this was valuable?

They did a premarital study. She did the workbook, but he did not. At the actual meetings, however, he discussed the study.

Did you participate in premarital counseling after engagement?

Yes, it was a six-month process. They met once a month with their counselors.

Were you a part of a study or Bible group? If so, when was this into the relationship?

He was already in a male group that met weekly. She started a women's Bible group within a few weeks of meeting him.

Were you a part of a weekly community group? If so, when was this into the relationship?

He had been in one about a year prior to their meeting; she was not part of a weekly community group.

Did you discuss what religion would look like in your family (e.g., go to church weekly or more than weekly; involvement of church in daily life and finances; if children would go to Christian schooling, etc.)?

It was a given, so they did not have to talk about what religion would look in their family. They knew they would be involved and active in their church. They did talk about schooling for the kids. Growing up, he went to private Christian school, and she was homeschooled.

When into the relationship did you discuss any obstacles or addictions that you needed to overcome? Was the elimination of these addictions expected? How were these problems resolved?

When they met, he dipped and drank alcohol occasionally. Colin was into brewing his own beer at the time. Eliza didn't date anyone who drank so he stopped for ten months. However, their church friends went out and socially drank occasionally (in a responsible way), so she eased up a bit. It was more important to her than it was to him. The obstacle they faced was his nicotine addiction. He promised her he stopped using nicotine, and she caught him two times. Through this, she learned how addictive nicotine could be. They were able to get through that time, and he does not use it anymore.

Throughout their dating, she noticed he was passionate about computers and assumed he was looking at porn. This was due to her experience in a prior relationship. He was open about his activity, and it turned out he was looking up codes and IT kind of stuff. He said in the interview that he wanted to start the relationship right and wanted to do the right thing in marriage. Because she always has been available, he never has fallen back on that.

PART IV - DAILY LIFE

As someone who romanticizes spending quality time together (*my* love language), hearing how much time Colin and Eliza shared both talking on the phone and in person was right up my alley. When meeting someone, it can be rougher even at the *beginning* of a relationship, not hearing from the other person consistently and wondering what they are thinking. Colin was generally the quiet type and could sum up a conversation fairly quickly. It amazed me this woman lit him with such a fire that he wanted to get to know more about her every day. Colin mentioned that he could not wait to see her and normally would tire of someone quickly. With her, it was different. He desired to know everything about her and that intense connection for her was new to him.

Did you speak daily early into the relationship? How long were your conversations at the beginning? When did this increase to a daily occurrence?

Yes, they spoke every day for hours by the end of the first week.

What type of communication was that generally more of—texting, phone conversations, FaceTime, in person, social media, etc.? How long typically were your conversations? How did your communication change as your relationship grew?

Communication between the two was primarily in person. They also texted all day long, spoke on the phone, and emailed each other. The longer emails started to go deeper as the relationship grew.

How many times a week did you see each other?

They saw each other seven days a week within the first couple of weeks of meeting.

When did you meet each other's core group of friends?

He did not have many friends other than his church community, which he was very active in. Colin met Eliza's friends early on, a few weeks into the relationship. However, he did not care for them since they were in a different place than he was, as he was a single father. She had not switched over to his church yet at that time. Once she did, she met new friends he liked through his church.

Did you discuss what type of movies to watch together? How did you handle it when one partner was uncomfortable with the content of the movie? What about TV shows, magazines, Internet activity?

They had different genres of movies they liked to watch. His were more violent, and they were married for several years before he finally stopped and watched different types of movies. If there were any uncomfortable scenes, they turned the movie off when dating and still do.

Did you go to each other's house? When watching movies or TV, did you lie down side by side, sit upright, or sit on separate couches?

Yes, they snuggled together when watching movies and primarily were at his house.

Did you have other friends of the opposite sex while dating? Did you agree that as you became more intimately involved, those relationships would need to change? How did you handle that? When into the relationship was this? How were those relationships changed?

Eliza had a few male acquaintances, but no one on an intimate level. Colin had a few female friends from college that were strictly platonic. They talked about avoiding those types of relationships and created boundaries with the opposite sex. At first she was not okay with his past. She would rip up old pictures of girls he had. She got through that and knows it was because she was insecure.

What were your boundaries with the opposite sex?

They agreed that neither of them would have lunch alone with their coworkers. When they were dating, neither of them really had a lot going on with the opposite sex.

Did you establish an open and safe conversation when one partner felt the other partner crossed the line with the opposite sex or made them feel uncomfortable?

> Eliza knew she had a flirty personality, and she became non-flirtatious. It was important to her to keep her attention focused on Colin.

Yes, open and safe conversations were welcome. They

did not have these issues with the opposite sex because they both were infatuated with one another. They also talked to the same people when they were together. Eliza knew she had a flirty personality, and she became non-flirtatious. It was important to her to keep her attention focused on Colin.

When did you introduce your spouse-to-be to your children? When did you allow them to establish a bond with the other person? How did you protect your children through this process?

After one month, she met his children. They dove in and involved them from the beginning. Once they knew they were in for the long haul (which was very early on), they became involved immediately.

PART V - SOCIAL MEDIA BOUNDARIES, EXPECTATIONS, AND ACCOUNTABILITY

Having issues of trust in my past, this part of the interview was both therapeutic and restorative. Knowing there was a man willing to open his trust at the beginning showed me that a man taking a relationship seriously would let you in completely. Colin knew what wounds of infidelity Eliza had in her past, and he was open to working through those. His actions showed her he could be trusted, right away. Sharing your life online, through phone, and on computer screens can reveal a person's integrity in moments. The instant Colin gave Eliza his passwords, he gave her the keys to his trustworthiness and character. The relationship was able to flourish from a well-laid foundation.

How did you keep each other accountable with social media while dating? Did this change after you were married?

He first found her on Myspace, and then Facebook took off. Immediately from the start they had each other's passwords. He doesn't like Facebook so does not have an account now. He gave her his password from week two, which really helped her heal from her past. They both had nothing to hide, there were no gray areas, there was no reason not to, and they were both on the same page.

Did you discuss how you would handle your social media interactions and accounts? If so, when into the relationship was this? Were you free to check each other's phone logs, text messages, emails, Facebook messages, Internet activity, and social media interactions, etc.?

From the start they were able to discuss any texts, phone logs, social media messages, etc. They both felt it was important to have access to all of each other's accounts. She looked through his texts and sometimes used his phone if she needed to do an online search for something. Her intently going through his phone lasted a few months.

Did you keep each other accountable on web browsing and viewing while dating? If you found something that made you feel uncomfortable, did you have open communication lines with your partner? What about after marriage?

They had open communication about web browsing and were able to talk about it anytime.

Were either of you "friends" with previous girlfriends or boyfriends on social media while dating? Did this affect the relationship? How was it handled?

Neither one of them had a former past relationship as friends on social media, so it was not an issue.

After marriage:

Do you have one social media account or separate ones?

He mainly uses Google Plus for business reasons, and she is on all his circles and sees what he posts. She has her own Facebook account, but he does not have one.

Do you share and discuss when others contact you on social media platforms?

They have not had much history around this because he does not like social media and she only uses Facebook. She always shares with him when someone contacts her but has not had any volatile people contact her.

Do you confront each other when you see a "like" or message that bothered you?

This has not been an issue for them but they feel comfortable saying something. They are always open about anything and discuss everything bluntly and honestly.

Internet activity: How do you keep each other accountable for this? Do you monitor each other, have a program that monitors it or have a friend that holds you accountable?

They have all of each other's passwords and access to any devices or accounts but do not monitor very closely anymore as their trust has grown. They do so much together and interact so much that it seems like it is unnecessary. For example, lying in bed at night, she will show him what she is reading, and then they will talk about it. Or he will mention something he stumbled across. Nothing is private and everything flows naturally like "two as one."

FINAL THOUGHTS FROM COLIN AND ELIZA

Eliza said: "Priorities, to have both in dating and in marriage. If you truly seek God above all else, He will guide you to the right person, and if you truly put God first and then each other first in dating as well as in marriage, purity in dating and connecting in marriage will really work. Also expectations, realistic expectations, allow for grace in the relationships. If you go into it thinking it's going to be a fairytale every day or a bed of roses, you will be disappointed and frustrated. If you realize it is hard work and you put in the effort to work through things, you will be pleasantly surprised at the beautiful things that come from it and will be content in the relationship."

Colin said: "Before you marry someone, ask yourself three questions—#1: Do they love Jesus? #2: Are they my best friend? #3: Can I see myself with them for the rest of my life?"

Colin and Eliza were a couple that showed sometimes a marriage does not look like what you may have imagined for yourself. Eliza never pictured herself married to a man who had been married before and who also had two daughters. A woman also never envisions herself meeting that man at a time when he is not financially prepared; they would need to sacrifice for a few years until it all came together. This couple beat those odds. Now they have found a way to live in harmony with the previous spouse, have a child of their own, and Colin is now at the height of his career. The once tiny home they started off in is now a rental, and they upgraded, now living in their dream home on the lake. They started off as best friends, and years later, it was nice to see that their marriage had grown stronger—spiritually, emotionally, and physically.

DISCUSSION QUESTIONS

- Are you open to a potential life partner having a situation you never pictured, such as if he or she already has children and/or had already been married?
- If infidelity has been a part of your story, what do you need upfront from the other person to help you through that? What boundaries do you need to set?
- How much quality time and communication do you desire from that person?

AIDEN AND REBEKAH: [SCREENSHOT]

MEET AIDEN AND REBEKAH:

AGES WHEN MARRIED:

Him: 30; Her: 32

LENGTH DATED:

10 months

LENGTH ENGAGED:

4 months

HOW LONG MARRIED NOW:

4 and a half years

LENGTH OF FIRST MARRIAGE:

He had been engaged prior once before

ANY CHILDREN PRIOR TO MARRIAGE:

No

HOW THEY MET:

They met on eHarmony. For Aiden, it had been a few years since he dated anyone. His options were limited as a Christian man, meaning he would primarily be looking for a spouse at church, work, or through friends. He chose eHarmony as he wanted a more filtered site. He signed up with a friend. He went on one or two dates before he got off for a six-month break as he felt like it wasn't getting anywhere. He got back on after his break. He realized that this time he needed to meet the woman he was talking to on eHarmony in person earlier in the relationship or it would fizzle out. He found his current wife a month later. He was not communicating with too many women. His radius was set farther at first and then reduced to 50-60 miles because he wanted to meet someone closer.

In her past, Rebekah had thought about eHarmony but knew of some friends that it did not turn out well for. She had previous guilt and fear about taking it out of God's hands so avoided it. A past friend was on the site and had a bad experience, and Rebekah did not want to feel guilty if it worked out for her. She had just gotten out of a relationship where the guy had been immature. Coming across Bianca Olthoff's blog one day, she found a post and video of her talking about eHarmony. Bianca is now married to a preacher, and they teach and travel the world and blog about love, life, and the pursuit of Jesus. Bianca was advising that you if decide to go online, to do it in community. She also was told by a friend that there is nothing to feel guilty about as it is just using the Internet as a tool; it is not interfering with someone you would meet outside of it. She emailed Bianca after they were dating, asking how Bianca and her husband handled being at different churches. Bianca wrote back saying their situation was a little different because they were both on staff at each church, so they would attend church at either location when time allowed. Rebekah was excited that

Bianca emailed her back, and later on she ended up meeting Bianca at a conference.

At the time, Rebekah was working at the church where she still attends and a coworker there would look with her through all of her matches. For the first month, nothing happened, and she was not going to renew her subscription. She prayed about it, but she didn't realize her profile was on auto-renew. Her radius was set to 50 miles, and she communicated with about four men. Finally, one last guy got in touch with her as she was about to give up; it was Aiden. She did not hear from him for a week, and then he said he was bad at this and asked to meet for coffee.

Sharing your gifts and talents with others is a gift in itself, and Rebekah exemplified how God wants us to share those.

Having met relationships online myself, and having most of my friends using online dating tools, I was eager to hear the insights from this couple. I met Rebekah through a women's study at church and noticed how kind, patient, and giving she was. There was a bride in our group who mentioned they were not able to have their wedding pictures taken, and Rebekah immediately offered to take them for free. I knew how expensive a photographer she was, so her offer was quite generous. The way she offered, so instantly, without wanting anything in return, was an attractive quality she possessed. Sharing your gifts and talents with others is a gift in itself, and Rebekah exemplified how God wants us to share those. Based on her character and the way she carried herself, I wanted to meet the man she married and find out more how their dating journey came about.

What attracted you to this person in the beginning?

Aiden thought Rebekah was pretty and liked the pictures she had on her profile. His favorite one was a professional shot that showed her looking up (she happened to be a photographer). He showed that picture to everyone. He also liked how even though it took him a week to write to her, she replied right back and did not hold it against him. Her reply was not passive-aggressive, spiteful, or edgy—that attracted him.

Rebekah liked that Aiden seemed to be a solid believer. She traveled a ton, and knowing that he had experiences with another culture was attractive to her. She also really liked one picture of him that made him look like a rock star. During the interview, even though they have been married four years, she pulled up his profile pics instantly that she had saved in a special spot on her phone. She still likes to look at them; they are some her favorites.

What characteristics were you looking for in your future partner?

He was looking for someone who he could share his life with. The *opposites attract* theory was not for him. They are both even-keeled; he needed someone who was not full with drama. Someone he knew he could be friends with was what he was looking for.

A godly man—he was actively pursuing a relationship with Christ, and that was important to her. He loved Christ more than he would love her. She wanted someone with goals, ambitions, and who was confident in who he was. She was also looking for someone she could have fun with.

Did he automatically lead from the start of contact? What did that look like? (woman's perspective)

Yes, Aiden was the one who sent Rebekah questions first on eHarmony. He asked her out first and was always intentional with questions to get to know her. At the end of the first date, he asked for her number. After that, it was hard for her to let him lead. She would want to start a text to him first and would stop herself and pray. Literally, she would get a text from him thirty minutes later. He also led her spiritually. They would listen to each other's podcasts and start discussions after listening to their church sermons.

What form of communication had been your primary one? Did you talk about if you prefer to text, see each other, or talk on the phone?

During the day, texting and emailing were the primary forms of communication. For Aiden, phone calls were more business and getting the details (what time to meet, where are they going to go, etc.), and then they would meet in person later. In person was their preference for communication.

When into the relationship did you discuss your intentions and expectations for the relationship? Who brought it up?

About five to six dates into the relationship, Rebekah had two weddings to shoot in one weekend. On her way to the second wedding, she remembered Aiden had called and asked to see her later that evening. That evening he talked to her to make sure she was clear about where they were. He told her he would let her know when he was ready to be in a relationship. She was relieved when he made his intentions clear. Part of the reason they needed to be clear about their relationship was that they were not being physically affectionate, which she could easily have interpreted as disinterest. That night clarified things for their relationship. Aiden did not want any assumptions being made.

A week after that, they went to dinner, and she was telling him about her past relationship. He was worried that she was hung up on her past. That night they told each other they were seeing each other exclusively; they were not checking their matches and closed out their eHarmony profiles.

When do you think you grew close to her? To him?

About five months into the relationship, they almost broke up. He told her he did not want to waste her time. He was trying to figure out what everything meant, so they took a week off. He needed time to evaluate what was going on. He was stewing on what was bothering him rather than talking about it. He recognized that he had to bring it up as he was keeping a mental list. Finally, he realized he needed to make a decision to move on. They sat down and talked, and he cried and told her how he was feeling. She was thrown off and didn't understand it. She asked Aiden if he had talked to anyone about his concerns. She was dating in community, and he was not. He was doing it alone and taking it upon himself. They almost broke up, but after they decided to stay together, he grew closer to her. She did not build a "you hurt me wall" and act differently toward him after that. He liked that forgiving spirit of hers.

After they worked through their *almost* breakup, Rebekah grew closer to him too. She knew fairly early on that she wanted to marry him. Hearing him talk during that time, she realized he had been holding back a lot and not voicing his expectations for the

> . . . she realized he had been holding back a lot and not voicing his expectations for the relationship.

relationship. They had great dates after they worked things out.

When did you first say I love you? Did you have the intention at that point for marriage?

She took the lead on this and shouldn't have. She was at a National Geographic photography workshop in San Francisco and went to a fortune cookie plant where she made several fortunes for him. This was about two and a half months into the relationship. Inside one of the fortunes was a paper that said "I love you." The others ones said something like "You are my sunshine," "I'm yours," and a Bible verse in another. The "I love you" fortune was the last one and he did not open it that night. She was relieved. However, she could not wait any longer and one night texted him to open the cookie that stated those words. He did not say it back. He was upset as he wanted to say it first. There was no pin-pointed moment when he said it back.

At what point in the relationship did you "know" you desired each other as your marriage partner? What was it that made you know? Was it a feeling or was something done?

After they took a week off, he grew close to her. Aiden fasted that week to get clarity. Initially, he wanted ten days to think about it, but Rebekah counter offered with three days, and they agreed on that. He emailed her and knew they needed to get together and talk. That's when he started to think about engagement.

He wanted to know all of these things about her, but she didn't want to open up if he was not going to be the one to marry her.

> . . . she didn't want to open up if he was not going to be the one to marry her.

They were both introverts, so it took practice and time. After their decision to move forward, they knew they needed mentors. When they met, they had no friends in common that knew them as a couple. Her church found a couple to meet with them as their mentor. This was seven months into the relationship.

For Rebekah, she knew Aiden was the one at Christmas. That was three months into the relationship.

Did you discuss what love language you responded to and when did you start acting upon that? Was this done before, during, or after the engagement?

Yes, they discussed it. He would come over to her house with three to four topics to "spark" conversation. One of them was the five love languages. She was not really into the topic. His was words of affirmation; hers was acts of service. Within the first couple of months, they had to have a few conversations about how they best communicate. They figured out their best way was through writing it down. He started a private blog where they could do entries to each other. He wanted it to be intentional and there to be a record. The only down side of the blog is that you could also see a "draft," but they trusted each other to not read the draft until it was posted for them to read.

Do you feel waiting for sexual intimacy sped up the dating process?

No, it was such a non-negotiable that it was not a factor. Sex was for after marriage, period. So they didn't play into that.

She felt the same way.

How hard was it to maintain the commitment before sexual intimacy?

It was difficult because they were attracted to each other, but they knew that sex was reserved for a marriage relationship so it was not on the table.

Did you discuss your sexual past or past partners, if any? When did you start to discuss this?

Yes, around month two or three. He wanted someone that had not had sex before but wanted to be realistic about expectations. He was not open to someone who had been married before or had children. He recognized that he was not mature enough to handle that.

She had also hoped he had not had sex before but knew at their age it would be hard to find someone like that. She also knew friends who had prior sexual relations and came to the Lord after that. She was open to meeting someone who had been married before and had children.

PART II - BOUNDARIES AND ACCOUNTABILITY

Aiden and Rebekah did one thing during this interview they probably were not aware of—touched each other constantly. I interviewed them while they were sitting on their couch as their newborn baby took a nap. They sat close to one another, and every time one of them spoke, the other one stared with a peaceful smile, as if quietly affirming, *that's my partner.* Aiden constantly reassured Rebekah during the interview, his hand either holding Rebekah's or stroking it softly, or with his arm around her shoulders and mixed in with a couple of sweet kisses. It was nice to see those moments between them as they reminisced their relationship and drew closer to each other.

Describe your first date:

Rebekah and Aiden met at Starbucks. He was super nervous and got there very early. She didn't like coffee, so as they ordered, she got a tea and spilled it because it was too full. He thought she didn't like him and got an awkward vibe. She wasn't being very inviting or looking him in the eye. But in reality, Rebekah was just trying to figure him out. Once they sat down, it went well and went by fast. They talked for a couple of hours and had plenty to talk about. After Starbucks closed for the night, he walked her to her car and asked her for her number. She flashed a big smile and that solidified for him they she liked him.

Did you establish boundaries from the get go? Who led that conversation?

They both talked about boundaries; it was an ongoing conversation.

What boundaries did you create? Did you have the same boundaries?

They tried a curfew at the beginning for 10 pm, and it worked for a little while. They went out a good bit, so it was outside of the house. They also did not spend nights at each other's house, except on two unique occasions. He had a hot tub in his backyard, and they didn't go into that together.

How did you hold each other accountable to those boundaries?

Reflecting back, they did not take full advantage of their resources and needed more accountability.

When did you start holding hands? What date was your first kiss?

He wanted to make sure they were going in the same direction and that she was comfortable with getting closer to him through holding hands and kissing. They were celebrating her birthday, and he asked her to be his *lady* instead of girlfriend. He held her hand then and kissed her for the first time. He was showing her his house for the first time, and they were out on his deck. This was two months into the relationship.

How did you control your sexual desires for each other? Did you discuss the difficulty of controlling your desire for each other?

It was hard to control. They discussed it. After they felt they had gone too far, they would set boundaries again.

Reflecting back, they did not take full advantage of their resources and needed more accountability.

Was this a local or long-distance relationship? Can you offer advice on long-distance relationships?

This was a local relationship. Their advice is not to stay at each other's place. He thinks the man should visit the woman more. She thinks she should meet his friends and see his lifestyle. Each should do an initial trip to see their environment; otherwise you are assuming a lifestyle and making it up in your head.

Did you ever spend the night at each other's house? Was this in the same bed? Were there other people in the house at the time? What was the situation?

Twice. The first time it was because they were going to NY the next day at 4 am. At that time, she slept in her bed, and he slept on the couch. The second time, it was raining outside, and they both accidentally fell asleep. It was not in the same bed, but on the same couch. They were both really tired and didn't even kiss.

Did you mainly do daytime dates? Did you do more group or one-on-one dating? Any overnight trips?

More evening dates and one-on-one. They went out to movies, restaurants, and wandered around downtown. They did a few outside movies on the lawn, which their downtown offered. They did one overnight trip by themselves to New York but had separate hotel rooms. Another time they went on a group trip to the mountains with her friends from college but also had separate rooms. The third overnight trip they had together was to go to DC to visit her mom, and again they had separate rooms.

At what point did you have a relationship and open discussions with his family, including seeing you involved as a part of the future family unit?

About two months into the relationship, Aiden met Rebekah's family in person (their first meeting was over Skype). Six months into the relationship, his parents came from out from the country and met her in person. Previously they had Skyped with her. Six months into the relationship, the conversation became more relaxed with them.

He met her mother two months into the relationship when they went to DC for Thanksgiving. Her father was deceased. Her mom talked to him about her ex-boyfriend, but her mother did not go too deep in conversation. She did not have too close of a relationship with her mother in that way.

Did you have a close person in your life that held you accountable, truly had your best interest in mind, and gave you advice?

Yes, they both did. Those people ended up being their best man and matron of honor.

PART III - A CHRIST-CENTERED RELATIONSHIP

When you are really connected to your church and involved heavily in its community, it becomes a part of you. For Rebekah to let Aiden lead the way in the area of which church to attend in their relationship showed her willingness to let him lead. That was an impressive part of the interview, as I wondered what you would do if you both loved your current church equally. In the end, it turned out just the way it was supposed to, but allowing her to take that leap of faith spoke volumes at that intricate moment in their relationship. Allowing Aiden to lead was a building block of other moments that would come in their relationship.

The first time you shared a meal, did he offer to bless the meal?

Yes.

Were you raised with the same religious backgrounds and values?

For the most part.

Did you come from the same faith or denomination?

They both came from Baptist backgrounds. His was more Fundamental, and hers was more Liberal. She changed to non-denominational in college, and he changed to non-denominational when he was twenty-five.

Did you attend the same church when you met? If not, whose church did you start attending, and when did you start attending together?

No, but before they got engaged, they had a conversation about it. Rebekah was more plugged in at her church and also worked there. He originally didn't want to switch to her church as it was a pride issue. He felt that she should go to his church. She really liked her church and wanted to stay at her church. She received counsel about leaving to go to his church and was guided that if he was being led in a Christian way, then it would be okay to change to his church. He needed her to say that she was willing to follow him. After that, they changed to her church.

When did you start praying together?

When they started dating officially, about two months into the relationship, they began praying together. But it was not on a regular basis.

Did you serve together while you were dating? Were they the same roles?

They served in different roles. He was on the video team at another church, and she was serving at her church in the student ministry.

Did you establish a mentor relationship with other strong Christian married couples while dating?

Yes, about six months into the relationship, they were placed with a mentor couple from her church and met with them once a month. That couple also gave them premarital counseling.

Did you do any type of workbook or study together? If so, when was this into the relationship? Did you think this was valuable?

He got the book *101 Questions to Ask Before You Get Engaged* by Norman Wright. They would ask each other questions on the way to dinner or email each other. He told her, "Don't think I'm going to get down on one knee at the end of the book though!"

Did you participate in premarital counseling after engagement?

Yes, they had four months of premarital counseling. She would have loved a spring wedding, but since they got engaged in July, they did not want to wait until the following spring. Their engagement may have been shorter, but the church's premarital counseling program was four months long so they opted for a four-month engagement and had a fall wedding.

Were you a part of a study or Bible group? If so, when was this into the relationship?

He was in a men's roundtable and *Quest for Authentic Manhood* study while they were dating. It was a big deal to be exposed to that teaching. It helped him lead more intentionally. She was going through the women's study *Biblical Femininity* when they first started dating.

Were you a part of a weekly community group? If so, when was this into the relationship?

She was in a weekly community group that she had been in for five years. He was also in one for six months at his church before he met her.

Did you discuss what religion would look like in your family (e.g., go to church weekly or more than weekly; involvement of church in daily life and finances; if children would have Christian schooling, etc.)?

A lot of that was assumed as they were going to similar churches. The 101 questions book went through that, so they were of one mind in that area.

When into the relationship did you discuss any obstacles or addictions that you needed to overcome? Was the elimination of these addictions expected? How were these problems resolved?

Neither of them had any obstacles or addictions. He had a protection called "Net Nanny" that would email his friend if he had gone on any inappropriate Internet sites and vice versa for his friend.

PART IV - DAILY LIFE

As a woman who gets fired up finding out other ways to keep engaged and communicated, discovering Aiden's blog was just as exciting to me as hearing about the shared Google calendar a few interviews before this one. Those two tips alone were worth having these interviews. Aiden had a more difficult time expressing his feelings toward Rebekah, and the blog allowed him the space to verbalize that. For Aiden to open up to Rebekah on that level was a large step toward a deeper connection and focus on marriage.

Did you speak daily early into the relationship? How long were your conversations at the beginning? When did this increase to a daily occurrence?

They did a lot of emailing at the beginning of the first month dating and during the week. Text was preferred, so they may have had four phone calls in six months. Back then he did not have unlimited texting, so he remembers he went way over on his bill.

What type of communication was that generally more of—texting, phone conversations, FaceTime, in person, social media, etc.? How long typically were your conversations? How did your communication change as your relationship grew?

They spoke more briefly on the phone and had more in-depth conversations through email and the private blog he created. Primarily they had face-to-face time with one-on-one dates.

How many times a week did you see each other?

They saw each other around four times a week.

When did you meet each other's core group of friends?

He met her college friends after a football game two months into the relationship. She met his friends on separate occasions around the two-month mark.

Did you discuss what type of movies to watch together? How did you handle it when one partner was uncomfortable with the content of the movie? What about TV shows, magazines, Internet activity?

He realized she did not like movies relying on a crass sense of humor, so they did not watch those movies together. If there is something inappropriate, he would turn his head in the theater or would fast forward that scene. If it was live TV, he would turn his head and look at her until it passed.

Did you go to each other's house? When watching movies or TV, did you lie down side by side, sit up right, or sit on separate couches?

Yes, and they would sit on the same couch, usually sitting up.

Did you have other friends of the opposite sex while dating? Did you agree that as you became more intimately involved, those relationships would need to change? How did you handle that? When into the relationship was this? How were those relationships changed?

She would have her friends' husbands as friends. He had to end a relationship with a girl that was a friend before he started dating. It would not have worked for him to remain friends with her and to date someone else.

What were your boundaries with the opposite sex?

Their first fight was over expectations of the understanding of very little one-on-one contact with the opposite sex. She had gone to a conference and went out with some new friends, two other girls and one guy. They were seated at the bar instead of a table, so she ended up talking with the guy while the other two girls chatted. They ended up talking about her faith, so she thought the conversation was cool. However, when she told him about it, he was not okay with her talking to some guy at a bar, no matter what the topic was about. That incident helped her understand what made him uncomfortable.

She had boundaries from learning while being on staff at the church. Some of those included to have the door open in meetings and to always have three people in a car at one time.

Did you establish an open and safe conversation when one partner felt the other partner crossed the line with the opposite sex or made them feel uncomfortable?

Yes, one guy who was a friend to her was texting her. She would tell Aiden about it. However, they don't recollect talking specifically about this. Aiden is the jealous one; Rebekah is not. He likes that she trusts him, but sometimes he would like for her to care more than she appears to.

PART V - SOCIAL MEDIA BOUNDARIES, EXPECTATIONS, AND ACCOUNTABILITY

Social media never seemed to be an issue with any of the couples interviewed, including Aiden and Rebekah. Openness, honesty, and transparency were a common thread among all the couples. They all shared a great deal with each other, nothing was a surprise to the other partner, and no areas were off limits or not talked about. Those were key components of keeping the strength in their fidelity and ongoing connection with each other.

How did you keep each other accountable with social media while dating? Did this change after you were married?

They didn't, and never felt the need to.

Did you discuss how you would handle your social media interactions and accounts? If so, when into the relationship was this? During courtship and engagements, were you free to check each other's phone logs, text messages, emails, Facebook messages, Internet activity, and social media interactions, etc.?

When they were dating, he found a bookmark about women who had been involved in pornography. He was super nervous to ask Rebekah about it, but since they had agreed to open communication, he asked her about it. The site ended up being bookmarked because of the ministry aspect of the website; she was not involved in any type of pornography. They did not have each other's computer passwords while dating.

Did you keep each other accountable on web browsing and viewing while dating? If you found something that made you feel uncomfortable, did you have open communication lines with your partner? What about after marriage?

She said her ex-boyfriend messaged her on Facebook, and she waited a while before telling Aiden. When the ex-boyfriend wanted to call her, she told Aiden about it. Now when an exchange like that happens, Rebekah shares it at that time instead of waiting.

Were either of you "friends" with previous girlfriends or boyfriends on social media while dating? Did this affect the relationship? How was it handled?

Yes, Aiden stopped following a previous girlfriend on Facebook once he and Rebekah started to date. Rebekah also unfriended her past boyfriends after they started dating.

After marriage:

Do you have one social media account or separate ones?

They each have a separate Facebook account and social media platforms.

Do you share and discuss when others contact you on social media platforms?

Yes, they have open communication and discuss anything needed. For example, an old guy friend asked an address for something local and Rebekah shared that with Aiden.

When someone messages that person through a social media channel, how is that handled?

They have open communication and don't hide anything.

Do you confront each other when you see a "like" or message that bothered you?

Yes.

Internet activity: How do you keep each other accountable for this? Do you monitor each other, have a program that monitors it, or have a friends that holds you accountable?

They have each other's log-on to their computers and have open communication. He used to have a program that monitored his activity prior to being married.

FINAL THOUGHTS FOR AIDEN AND REBEKAH

"Wait for the Lord, be strong and take heart and wait for the Lord" (Psalm 27:14).

> "Wait for the Lord, be strong and take heart and wait for the Lord" (Psalm 27:14).

From the Rebekah's point of view: "Trust me when I say that it's difficult to be single. I waited thirty-two years for the right man. But walking that road strengthened my faith and drew me closer to the Lord in many different seasons of singleness. Watching others take relationships into their own hands and those situations not work out (whether through a breakup or difficult marriage) only solidified for me the reasons to wait for the man God had for me. I would rather be single the rest of my life than to be with the wrong person, a thousand times over!"

Aiden's perspective: "Don't settle for someone just so you aren't alone. Wait for the right person, a godly person that God has in mind for you. And listen to the advice of friends and family in regards to who you are dating. They have your best interest in mind and also have a more objective point of view and are able to see things that you may have become blind to."

My takeaways from Aiden and Rebekah were quite helpful not only for myself but also for me to pass along to others. Having an accountability partner with someone you trust when using online sites as a tool to help you meet other people was a valuable tip. Your trusted source can see things you may not otherwise, guide you, and keep you on track.

DISCUSSION QUESTIONS

- If you have not selected an accountability partner yet, who would that be? How often should you check in with them?
- What are your boundaries with someone if using an online dating site? Are you doing this in community or by yourself?
- Are you open to attending your partner's church while dating?
- If your partner expresses themselves better in writing, are you open to that also?

ETHAN AND SARA: [SECOND CHANCES]

MEET ETHAN AND SARA:

AGES WHEN MARRIED:

Him: 46; Her: 47

LENGTH DATED:

6 months

LENGTH ENGAGED:

6 months

HOW LONG MARRIED NOW:

11 years

LENGTH OF FIRST MARRIAGE:

Him: 16 years; Her: 20 years

ANY CHILDREN PRIOR TO MARRIAGE:

Him: 3 children; Her: 2 children

HOW THEY MET:

Through the singles group at church. However, they met one year prior at a Christian singles dance without even realizing it at the time. Ethan also went to a Valentine's Day function and saw Sara there. She was a part of the hospitality committee, so he noticed she was at the same places he was. They were both seeing other people at the time, but it was not the right fit for either of them. Her singles group pastor sat her down twice to tell her the guy she was seeing at the time was not the right man for her.

Sara met me at a very low point in my life. In fact, meeting her is one of the reasons this book was created in the first place. Sara was my Christian counselor when I needed guidance the most. Her openness and vulnerability was something I was so grateful for. She shared such personal things with me that I felt comfortable sharing my situation with her at that time and held nothing back.

Through Sara's sharing of her past and how she got through it and also seeing what blessings she currently had was a light I so desperately needed when we met. I've kept in touch with Sara over the years here and there. Seeing and being with her is bittersweet as it sometimes triggers a painful time in my life, but it also reminds me why God placed her in my life. I have always known my worth, but she encouraged me and showed me deeper ways to exemplify what a Christian woman is.

It was difficult taking on some of Sara's advice at the time, as it required me to be patient and go against my natural controlling-type nature. God had other plans for me, and He let me be guided by Sara and then revealed the brighter future He had planned for me instead.

I knew bits and stories of her and Ethan's relationship but was ready to dive in for some details. I thought so highly of Sara; her presence itself will light up a room. She is truly a burst of sunshine with the wisest of words. Whenever I had doubts about what's yet to come, sometimes I would pull out the card she mailed to me and read the words and Scripture she wrote out for me. They calm me in an instant and refresh my spirit.

I'd briefly met Ethan at church and looked forward to learning more about their relationship. After hearing about their stories and observing how restored she was, I craved to know the details on how he captured her heart, what boundaries they set, and how she was able to love again.

What attracted you to this person in the beginning?

Ethan was physically attracted to Sara. He just knew she was different, and she stood out in his mind. He was dating someone else at that time, but they were more like friends. They had dated one year and were there for each other when he needed that, but he knew that woman wasn't the one.

The minute Ethan walked into singles group at church, Sara thought "what a hunk of burning love." He shared his story on forgiveness in front of the group, and that also attracted her to him.

What characteristics were you looking for in your future partner?

Someone who was loving and kind to his kids. (She latched on to them at the beginning.) It was an added bonus that Sara was pretty. Ethan wanted a godly woman and said she didn't have a mean bone in her body. He is blessed to have her in his life and spend every day with her.

She was looking for a godly man and spiritual leader. She was growing at the time with her journey. She wanted someone to be her best friend, who loved the outdoors and was adventurous. She liked how she could even just go to the trash dump with him and have fun.

Did he automatically lead from the start of contact? What did that look like? (woman's perspective)

Yes, he opened the door on the first date and prayed with her at meals. She liked that he was a man with a plan. She had to adjust to the idea of being with someone after being single for so long and living as a very independent woman. She had to learn to let him lead and wasn't used to having a spiritual leader. If she didn't agree with something, she would go to the Lord and pray about it.

What form of communication had been your primary one? Did you talk about if you prefer to text, see each other, or talk on the phone?

Seeing each other in person was their primary form of communication, although they utilized other forms of communication as well, including email, cards, and phone calls.

When into the relationship did you discuss your intentions and expectations for the relationship? Who brought it up?

Two months into the relationship, on Christmas Day, he wrote her a letter and put it in a Christmas card. She was concerned it was too fast and wondered if she was on the rebound as she had recently gotten out of a two-year relationship. He mentioned that even if it didn't work out, he wanted God's best for her. That sealed the deal for her. He wanted a courtship, not a dating experience. He had stayed celibate for six years, so was not looking for a fling and just dating. He was not going shopping around by attending the single Christian functions or going on the Internet. He was attending those functions and the singles group more to find other Christian male friends.

When do you think you grew close to her? To him?

It was from the start for him. It was as if God had ordained it and he knew her for years. For her it was when he came to see her in the ER on Christmas Day. She had gotten very sick and had to go to the hospital, and he came to sit with her and be with her even though he had his family to be with also. He took her to pick up her prescriptions and gave her that letter that day and shared his intentions.

When did you first say I love you? Did you have the intention at that point for marriage?

The first time he kissed her, in mid-December, Ethan told Sara that he loved her. She looked like an angel to him that night at dinner. He had not felt that way since he was a kid. Their dating was like God gave them the opportunity to start over and do it right. She did not say those words back to him that night. It was after she received the letter, and she was scared she was going to screw up again and mess it up.

At what point in the relationship did you "know" you desired each other as your marriage partner? What was it that made you know? Was it a feeling or was something done?

At the four-month mark, Ethan knew he wanted Sara as his marriage partner and called her daughter and son to ask for her hand in marriage. He asked her daughter for her ring size. He had no idea where to go, and God led him to a jewelry store. The owners ended up going to their church. The owner asked if Ethan wanted quality or quantity. He said quality. It was just a feeling that made him know; it was God-ordained. He proposed one month later.

Three months into the relationship, there was an ice storm. She was stranded at his house and had to spend the night on the couch. The fireplace was nearby, and it was hot, so he opened the top few buttons of his shirt (not intentionally for her to see), exposing his chest—she wanted him at that moment. The passion drove her. There was a lot of chemistry and passion in addition to the awesome qualities he exhibited.

The passion drove her. There was a lot of chemistry and passion in addition to the awesome qualities he exhibited.

Did you discuss what love language you responded to, and if so, when did you start acting upon that? Was this done before, during, or after the engagement?

They dove into the five love languages more after the marriage. They did a study of it in their church group but didn't really talk about it.

Do you feel waiting for intimacy sped up the dating process?

Sex was not the reason they got married. They were physically attracted to each other, but it was not a driving force.

How hard was it maintaining the commitment before intimacy?

He had waited a long time already, and he did not want to dishonor her. Also, if he had sex with her prior to marriage, he thinks it would have broken them up. He always had a piece of him that regretted not waiting until he got married the first time. He knew she was God's daughter and thought who was he to violate her?

Did you discuss your sexual past or past partners, if any? When did you start to discuss this?

She shared her salvation story with him within their first month—that was one of the things that attracted him. He shared that he was waiting to be intimate until marriage in the beginning. He wanted to show her early on that it included having those boundaries. He can't pinpoint the exact moment; it may have been discussed in the singles group.

PART II - BOUNDARIES AND ACCOUNTABILITY

After he met Sara, he formed a friendship with her first and then led her with an intentional heart.

Listening to Ethan's past experiences, I admired the way he celebrated his singleness and focused on being a father before Sara came into his life. After he met Sara, he formed a friendship with her first and then led her with an intentional heart. Hearing the way he connected with her in the morning through his letters, checked in on her during the afternoon, and yearned to see her after work was a pursuit I had longed for. Ethan exemplified the type of leadership most women search for by establishing boundaries upfront, sharing his feelings toward her, and having accountability partners in their life.

Describe your first date:

The Lord laid on his heart to call her and ask her to go up to the mountains and see the color change. They went to Brevard and went to a fall street festival. He can actually picture where he parked and the vendor booths. They went to an old-fashioned soda shop and ate hamburgers by a Route 66 sign. It was the perfect day; it was so comfortable and natural. Neither of them was nervous. They felt like best friends and compatible. They did a little hike on the way back, and then later that night they had to go to a birthday party. The next day they met at church, and then she was waiting for her daughter to have a baby.

Prior to their actual first date by themselves, they had hung out a few times in church groups. They had a singles tea at church one time, and he was assigned to serve her table as the men were waiting on the ladies. She was actually dating someone else at that time. She noticed at the end, because she was on the hospitality team, that he asked if he could help pack the tea up. She was not used to a man offering to help like that; it was what she was looking for. On another occasion, the church group went ice skating and also took children from an orphanage skating. She had him "show her" how to ice skate—it was the first time they touched at all, but before they started dating. She also saw that day how he treated children and had not seen that from the man she was dating at that time.

Did you establish boundaries from the get go? Who led that conversation?

They discussed boundaries early on, and he led that conversation.

What boundaries did you create? Did you have the same boundaries?

Mainly not to have overnight stays. They only did that once, during an ice storm as it was too dangerous to drive, and she slept on the couch. Even on the day he proposed, they drove down to the beach just for the day, which was around five hours away. He proposed, they rode bikes on the beach, had a celebratory dinner, and got back home at 2 am. They were very clear with each other about their boundaries.

How did you hold each other accountable to those boundaries?

They were committed to do it God's way and not have sex before marriage. He would get up and leave her house if he felt out of control. Early on they had a friend that chaperoned their dates and provided that accountability.

When did you start holding hands? What date was your first kiss?

Their first kiss was the same day as the first time they held hands, two months into the relationship. After that, it never stopped.

How did you control your sexual desires for each other? Did you discuss the difficulty of controlling your desire for each other?

They did not spend the night. They set a clear boundary to wait until marriage to have intercourse. He had to leave early sometimes, and they just had to stop. Yes, they let each other know that it was hard to control.

Was this a local or long-distance relationship? Can you offer advice on long-distance relationships?

This was a local relationship. Their advice is to be cautious with long-distance relationships as it can be dangerous. Without interaction in person, it can be easy to get invested emotionally via texting, phone calls, emails, etc. This does not allow you the opportunity to look objectively. Someone can hide things well because quality time is not there. A connection could be made without truly knowing that person. Just know time is your friend.

Did you ever spend the night at each other's house? Was this in the same bed? Were there other people in the house at the time? What was the situation?

One time, during the ice storm. His children were in the house, and she slept on the couch.

Did you mainly do daytime dates? Did you do more group or one-on-one dating? Any overnight trips?

More evening, one-on-one dates were done. They met for supper, rode bikes, and enjoyed other light activities. He had two kids living with him, so he had to get home at night. They had one overnight trip to Arizona to visit his family.

At what point did you have a relationship and open discussions with his family, including seeing you involved as a part of the future family unit?

Her kids encouraged the relationship early on. She recalls that one time when she turned down a date with him so she could pull her weeds, her kids told her she could do that another time and to go on the date! The talked to each other's kids ongoing throughout the relationship, mainly at the kitchen table at night. The most serious conversation held was when he asked her daughter for her mom's hand in marriage.

They flew to Arizona to meet his mother ten months into the relationship; they were engaged at that point. His mother had thirty yellow roses waiting for her at the airport when they met.

Did you have a close person in your life that held you accountable, truly had your best interest in mind, and gave you advice?

Yes, it was a lady that was in the singles group at church. She would check in with them and go to the movies with them when they were doing group dating before they moved to primarily one-on-one dating.

PART III - A CHRIST-CENTERED RELATIONSHIP

The most unforeseen answer came from both Ethan and Sara when they mentioned they were not saved until their adult years. I automatically assumed they had been practicing Christians their entire lives and just got off track. It was eye-opening to learn it was much later, and what a joy it was to hear the difference in the way they dated with a Christ-centered focus after they were saved.

The first time you shared a meal; did he offer to bless the meal?

Yes.

Were you raised with the same religious backgrounds and values?

No, he did not go to church growing up. She went to church every Sunday.

Did you come from the same faith or denomination?

No, he was saved at twenty-four years old. She was raised Catholic and saved at forty-two. He was the first one in his family to be saved.

Did you attend the same church when you met? If not, whose church did you start attending and when did you start attending together?

No, they were at different churches. He was just going to the singles group at her church. Ethan started to attend her church less than a year before they started dating. By the time they began dating, they were both attending the same church.

When did you start praying together?

Immediately at meal time and then over certain situations.

Did you serve together while you were dating? Were they the same roles?

No. She was volunteering at the Children's Home (an orphanage) and also leading in ladies' Bible groups and on the hospitality team. He was not serving at that time.

Did you establish a mentor relationship with other strong Christian married couples while dating?

Yes, they had a premarital mentor couple and also one after engagement.

Did you do any type of workbook or study together? If so, when was this into the relationship? Did you think this was valuable?

They both did studies in their singles groups. This was valuable as more in-depth conversations happened at breakout groups during those times and they got to know each other through that.

Did you participate in premarital counseling after engagement?

Yes, for six weeks.

Were you a part of a study or Bible group? If so, when was this into the relationship?

She led a women's group and study. He met with two guys from Sunday school every Saturday for a study and accountability group.

Were you a part of a weekly community group? If so, when was this into the relationship?

They were both in the singles group, meeting regularly and doing studies through that group.

Did you discuss what religion would look like in your family (e.g., go to church weekly or more than weekly; involvement of church in daily life and finances; if children would go to Christian schooling, etc.)?

Yes, they knew exactly what they wanted together. They talked about serving together. They are now premarital counselors and talk about saving a marriage before it starts. She had a book by Dr. Leslie Parrott that asked a similar question about what she desired with her spouse. The answer she wrote down at the time was to be a premarital counselor, small group leader, and minister to grandchildren. She can look back at what she wrote down, and she is now doing all three.

When into the relationship did you discuss any obstacles or addictions that you needed to overcome? Was the elimination of these addictions expected? How were these problems resolved?

Neither had addictions—except to each other! They had nothing to hide from one another. Her concern was that she was raising someone else's children. The realization didn't really dawn on her until after they were married.

PART IV - DAILY LIFE

Ethan and Sara enjoyed every night together, spending time at the dinner table and being thankful they found each other. The way they connected daily was sweet to hear about; they were not going to let a moment go by without learning more about each other and enjoying the journey toward a lifetime together.

Did you speak daily early into the relationship? How long were your conversations at the beginning? When did this increase to a daily occurrence?

Every night they saw each other for about two to three hours. This occurred fairly quickly, after their first official date.

What type of communication was that generally more of—texting, phone conversations, FaceTime, in person, social media, etc.? How long typically were your conversations? How did your communication change as your relationship grew?

In person was their primary communication. They enjoyed more in-depth and very open conversations. He would email her every morning. When she got to work she would have an email from him, and she looked forward to getting those. He would call to check in with her at work to make plans for later that evening. They both would send each other cards in the mail; she loved sending him a ton of cards. He gave her a white gift bag and put just a little something small in it. She returned the bag with a surprise, and it started their gift bag exchange. They used the same small white bag and swapped it back and forth. It would be filled with random items from golf balls, candy, a CD, a part for a bike, and so forth, and neither one ever knew when they would get the bag back. It was swapped every three to four weeks. One hundred days before their wedding, she filled a jar with one hundred Hershey's Kisses. Each day he ate a kiss, and he ate the last one on their wedding day.

How many times a week did you see each other?

They saw each other every night except one night. She drove up to his house, and it was dark. He wasn't answering his phone, so she found out later he fell asleep.

When did you meet each other's core group of friends?

Her core group of friends in their singles group became his friends too. This group of people were who they generally hung out with. She did introduce him to a few of her couple friends from her past marriage around six months into dating, and they still hang out with them today. She did meet a few of his friends early on, around three months.

Did you discuss what type of movies to watch together? How did you handle it when one partner was uncomfortable with the content of the movie? What about TV shows, magazines, Internet activity?

They monitored what they watched and usually watched something light like *So you Think They Can Dance, Survivor, Elf,* etc. If a movie or show used the Lord's name in vain or was sexual in nature, they would turn it off or change the channel. They were both really into one show, but it started to become too inappropriate, so they stopped watching it. They do not Internet surf a lot.

Did you go to each other's house? When watching movies or TV, did you lie down side by side, sit up right, or sit on separate couches?

Yes, they both went to each other's house. They would snuggle on the couch and lie side by side.

Did you have other friends of the opposite sex while dating? Did you agree that as you became more intimately involved, those relationships would need to change? How did you handle that? When into the relationship was this? How were those relationships changed?

Neither of them had friends of the opposite sex.

He makes sure to make decisions that would never cause jealous feelings in her.

What were your boundaries with the opposite sex?

She works with all men and never has lunch alone with them. He is in the contracting business so is in the homes of a lot of women. They have trust in each other. It is a character issue and understanding of that trust. He makes sure to make decisions that would never cause jealous feelings in her.

Did you establish an open and safe conversation when one partner felt the other partner crossed the line with the opposite sex or made them feel uncomfortable?

Crossing the line never happened as the trust was there and he would not let those conversations with the opposite sex go on long enough to make her feel uncomfortable. That is still always a conscious decision he is making.

When did you introduce them to your children? When did you allow them to establish a bond with the other person? How did you protect your children through this process?

On the first Thanksgiving, Sara didn't know if she should invite Ethan to Thanksgiving with her kids. The kids were teenagers, and they said they were okay, but they wanted to be respectful of them. One month later at Christmas, she met his kids.

PART V - SOCIAL MEDIA BOUNDARIES, EXPECTATIONS, AND ACCOUNTABILITY

How did you keep each other accountable with social media while dating? Did this change after you were married?

They were not Facebook users then; they had instant messaging so used that instead and did not text each other.

Did you discuss how you would handle your social media interactions and accounts?

Internet activity was not an issue while they were dating; they did not use the above social platforms at that time.

Did you keep each other accountable on web browsing and viewing while dating? If you found something that made you feel uncomfortable, did you have open communication lines with your partner? What about after marriage?

This is applicable after marriage. She is more actively involved now.

Were either of you "friends" with previous girl/boyfriends on social media while dating? Did this affect the relationship? How was it handled?

No.

After marriage:

Do you have one social media account or separate ones, e.g., Facebook, Instagram, Pinterest board, etc.?

They have individual Facebook accounts. She is more actively involved than he is.

Do you share and discuss when others contact you on social media platforms?

Sometimes high school friends will post something, and she will tell him. If she receives a private message, she always tells him about it.

When someone messages that person through a social media channel, how is that handled?

They would tell each other about it; she is primarily the one online now.

Do you confront each other when you see a "like" or message that bothered you?

Nothing is hidden; they communicate with each other.

Internet activity: How do you keep each other accountable for this? Do you monitor each other, have a program that monitors it, or have a friends that holds you accountable?

They both have each other's passwords to everything. Sometimes he will ask her to look something up in his email account. She keeps her Facebook open, and all activity can be seen. He also knows her character so trusts her.

FINAL THOUGHTS FROM ETHAN AND SARA

"Put God in the center. So many people want to give up. Serve and be a servant."

Ethan and Sara mirrored the type of relationship I hoped for—quality time together with a marriage-minded focus. The way Ethan rose up early in the morning to make sure his was the first message in Sara's inbox and his eagerness to visit with her each evening made me smile. His love for her was apparent, and he was genuinely appreciative that God brought them together. Sara was cautious of her heart this time around, but Ethan proved that he was the man for her day after day. Coming to care for her in the ER during Christmastime was a big win for me, and it was a joy listening to them. Even though I met Sara during a turbulent time, God used her to show me that I can also have grace and be blessed with an amazing man like she was. I thank Sara for every night she met with me. She truly made a difference in my life.

DISCUSSION QUESTIONS

- Who has made a difference or been influential in your life during a tough time? What did you learn out of that?
- What house or overnight boundaries have you set for yourself?
- Would you like a third person on your first few dates like Ethan and Sara or prefer more one-on-one dates?
- What did you learn from Ethan and Sara about second chances and dating through a godly focus?

CONCLUSION

Faithful boundaries allow you the opportunity to reveal and explore with each other who you are without the emotional and physical connections overlooking some critical characteristics of that person.

It is refreshing to know married partners who set and held firm to physical, emotional, and spiritual boundaries before making a marriage covenant. These couples set the stage for a finding a more compatible person to be their marriage partner. It is written there will be trouble in marriages (Cor. 7:28) and having an equally yoked mate is vital when enduring the trenches of life. Faithful boundaries allow you the opportunity to reveal and explore with each other who you are without the emotional and physical connections overlooking some critical characteristics of that person. If you are not overly intimate—emotionally, physically, or spiritually—with that person before it is time, it will be a lot easier to exit if necessary when you notice they have a severe temper several months later, when you discover they have a wandering eye you did not know about, when you learn they do not want children, or when they are caught lying.

A few months typically reveal what you previously were unaware of; they are no longer on their best behavior. Their natural, comfortable self is exposed. It can be eye-opening. Opening your heart at a parallel level with your partner gives you clarity and a different perspective. It allows you to live in each other's daily lives and witness how each responds when that person is tired, angry, self-doubting, challenged, feeling unloved, pressured at work, or frustrated emotionally and physically. How involved is that person with their faith? Are they simply going to church but only living parts of the Word that are comfortable to *them*? Life will throw a myriad of obstacles and hurdles along the way, and this is your opportunity to view firsthand how they respond. What are their actions when you are sick? If a pet or loved one dies or is ill? If you lose your job or they lost theirs? How has their past affected their present? How do they communicate or handle confrontation? Are they financially stable and emotionally mature? How much of their time are they giving you and as a couple? How do they handle relationships with the opposite sex? How do your future plans align? Do your family and friends think you are a good fit? Are your daily lives compatible? With a myriad of questions to ask, there is one thing that must occur: communication.

Without communication and really getting to know that person before both making a marriage decision, sometimes lust can make the decision instead. In the beginning is a perfect time for group gatherings, shepherding from other Christian couples, lots of coffee talks, serving together, family time, activities like walks, hiking, cooking, and just plain sitting down and communicating.

While getting to know each other, share yourselves at equal amounts. If one partner has stopped showing increasing action of moving forward and putting more into the developing relationship, then stop sharing, re-evaluate, and make a decision. This can be easily felt and visually seen through lack of action of fewer texts or phone calls, decreased efforts of carving time for one another, less sharing of information, less talk of the future, less effort and action steps from one partner, and decreased excitement over that other person in general. The difficult part is when one person starts to feel more than the other. It is overwhelmingly tempting to wait and see and bend over backwards to please the other person. You can easily get desperate to win their affection. But just—stop. Back off. Be honest of your expectations, needs, and goals in a Christian manner. Many times we are terrified to be honest and ask tough questions in fear of loss. In reality, the loss will have already been there before the question is answered. The answer was just delayed.

God can be using a situation to *change you*, not that circumstance or that person. He is developing your biblical character. You are the one being tested—your behaviors and your choices. If that other person is not sharing those same biblical views, then be patient and wait for the one who does.

You should not have to convince a potential mate to attend church with you; they should be willing to go, no questions asked. The process should be simple and easy. It should also involve effort, not excuses. Their behavior will dictate their care and love.

When you enter a relationship with one person, other relationships will need to be redefined or possibly let go. You are gaining gratification from one person with God in the center rather than unfulfillment from multiple sources, as those can leave you with a false sense of relationship. The letting go of those other types of connections opens the door for one complete wholeness with another person.

To simplify, you may not get to have lunch alone, talk to, or send text messages to certain persons in your life without your partner in the room. In return, now you get to do those with your chosen partner, one who gives you complete love, honesty, and emotional investment in return. You are also allowing that other person(s) you once shared those experiences with to give their partner their best and loyalty, creating a cycle of biblical principles. By your choice and discipline to disengage, essentially you redirect them to their chosen partner through your behavior.

When it is all over, what do you do when left crushed in spirit, body, and heart? Where do you look for that godly partner?

You pray to your Heavenly Father for redemption, grace, mercy, and wisdom. Then you simply begin again and start your search. He will renew your spirit and your heart and double your blessings.

He will repay you for the time lost to Him.

As for looking for that godly partner, God also gives clarity there. Let it be His responsibility to show you that person.

God's Word is God's protection. Your free will is not free, as every choice has its consequences. It is up to you to decide whether you want positive or negative ones. However, those set boundaries may be different for every couple. May this book help you along your way to finding your partner with holiness, faithfulness, and obedience, with God's Word at the center.

"Your greatest ministry will flow out of your pain—not out of your strengths or your talents but out of the painful experiences of your life. It is your weaknesses that help other people in their need, not your strengths."

~ Rick Warren

RECOMMENDED READING

HOLDING HANDS, HOLDING HEARTS – RICHARD AND SHARON PHILLIPS

This book is dear to my heart. After reading the book, I was curious about the authors and overjoyed to learn they live in my very own city. Both Richard and Sharon graciously met with me to share their wisdom and advice about seeking a spouse, what to include in the book, and marriage itself. Richard pointed out after speaking with me that I kept mentioning patience and should include that in the book. He was able to pinpoint the weakness I struggled with at that time, and I am grateful for that, as it allowed me to recognize that weakness and work daily to rely on faith instead. But most of all, he ended the meeting with not only praying over this book but also praying for my husband. I will never forget being in the room with this preacher and his wife as they held my hands over the table and prayed the most sincere, open, and direct prayer to God. It was a much cherished moment to me. Two pieces that stuck with me from the book include: "A man may exude confidence without a godly character. A foolish woman swoons over a charming man without considering whether she is safe in his hands." Additionally: "One of the reasons why so many fall into sexual sin—bringing guilt into the relationship and short-circuiting its emotional and spiritual growth—is that they place themselves in tempting situations. This is simply foolish, and Christian men and women who are realistic about sexual temptation will not put themselves in a position to fall."

SEX, DATING, AND RELATIONSHIPS – GERALD HIESTAND AND JAY THOMAS

Gerald and Jay are straight shooters in this book, and their plain spokenness is refreshing. Their references to Paul and Corinthians are spot on and sum it up when they state, "The implications are clear: the marriage relationship is the only legitimate context for sexual relations."

THE SACRED SEARCH – GARY THOMAS

Can this person walk with me toward God? This is one of the important questions Gary suggests we ask ourselves when choosing a marriage partner wisely. He lays it out there and addresses, in his words, "discerning someone's character, true values, and suitability for marriage is hard work. It takes time, counsel, and a healthy dose of objective self-doubt and skepticism." Gary's helpful study questions following each chapter allows us the opportunity to find out if both partners are building on the same foundation.

WILD AT HEART – JOHN ELDREDGE

As a woman, this book intrigued me as I wanted to learn more about men from a man's perspective. It reminded me about the wildness of a man, but it was also comforting to view through the author's lens that a man can offer both strength *and* passion in a godly manner. I encourage all women to read this book and delve into understanding the male perspective on a richer and often misunderstood level.

BIBLICAL FEMININITY – GRACE CHURCH AND EDITED BY CHRYSTIE COLE

Not only have I had the pleasure of reading this book, but I was able to do the women's study group and separately meet Chrystie Cole. Both have been impactful in the writing of this book. A line I hold dear to my heart is, "But when a woman entrusts her heart to Christ rather than withdrawing into self-protection, she is free to bare herself to another in a way that assists them in their mission." Chrystie also states, "She is humble and does not know what is best for her. She knows that she may not love the season she is in, but she can trust and obey God in it. Because of this belief, she does not turn in on herself in despair and frustration; she continues to live with a posture of gratitude and humility."

SAFE PEOPLE – DR. HENRY CLOUD AND DR. JOHN TOWNSEND

I lit this book up like wildfire with my multi-colored note tabs. Cloud and Townsend offer advice we all know deep down inside, but reading it on the pages reminds us what to look for in a partner. A few of my highlighted lines included the following:

"Unsafe people demand trust instead of earning it;" "If, like Jesus, we are truly trustworthy, we would welcome questioning from our loved ones on our 'trustability.' We would want others to see our deeds and actions, that they would feel more comfortable. We would want to know what gives them suspicion or fear and try to do everything to allay those fears."

SEX AND DATING – MINDY MEIER

Mindy excels at assisting others getting through what they need to get through. She reminds us that God has the ability to heal the broken-hearted, and there is hope. This one line in her book was so strong it practically summed up the reason I wrote this book. "Many times the pain of a broken romance is what prompts us to come to Christ, either in rebirth or in recommitment. Through suffering we can gain new perspective on what's important in life."

SCRIPTURE

IN YOUR SEARCHING SEASON AND IN MARRIAGE

"He who finds a wife finds what is good and receives favor from the LORD."

~ Proverbs 18:22 (NIV)

"Houses and wealth are inherited from parents, but a prudent wife is from the LORD."

~ Proverbs 19:14 (NIV)

"Treat younger men as brothers, older women as mothers, and younger women as sisters, with absolute purity."

~ 1 Timothy 5:1b-2 (NIV)

"Now to the unmarried and the widows I say: It is good for them to stay unmarried, as I do. But if they cannot control themselves, they should marry, for it is better to marry than to burn with passion."

~ 1 Corinthians 7:8–9 (NIV)

"Flee from sexual immorality. All other sins a person commits are outside the body, but whoever sins sexually, sins against their own body. Do you not know that your bodies are temples of the Holy Spirit, who is in you, whom you have received from God? You are not your own; you were bought at a price. Therefore honor God with your bodies."

~ 1 Corinthians 6:18–20 (NIV)

"Marriage should be honored by all, and the marriage bed kept pure, for God will judge the adulterer and all the sexually immoral."

~ Hebrews 13:4 (NIV)

"But I tell you that anyone who looks at a woman lustfully has already committed adultery with her in his heart."

~ Matthew 5:28 (NIV)

"Nevertheless, in the LORD woman is not independent of man, nor is man independent of woman. For as woman came from man, so also man is born of woman. But everything comes from God."

~ 1 Corinthians 11:11–12 (NIV)

"Since they are no longer two, but one flesh. Therefore what God has joined together, let no one separate."

~ Matthew 19:6 (NIV)

"Now flee from youthful lusts and pursue righteousness, faith, love *and* peace, with those who call on the LORD from a pure heart."

~ 2 Timothy 2:22 (NASB)

"For this is the will of God, your sanctification; *that is,* that you abstain from sexual immorality; that each of you know how to possess his own vessel in sanctification and honor, not in lustful passion, like the Gentiles who do not know God; *and* that no man transgress and defraud his brother in the matter because the Lord is *the* avenger in all these things, just as we also told you before and solemnly warned *you.* For God has not called us for the purpose of impurity, but in sanctification. So, he who rejects *this* is not rejecting man but the God who gives His Holy Spirit to you."

~ 1 Thessalonians 4:3–8 (NASB)

INSTRUCTION ON MARRIAGE

"Now regarding the questions you asked in your letter. Yes, it is good to abstain from sexual relations. But because there is so much sexual immorality, each man should have his own wife, and each woman should have her own husband.

"The husband should fulfill his wife's sexual needs, and the wife should fulfill her husband's needs. The wife gives authority over her body to her husband, and the husband gives authority over his body to his wife.

"Do not deprive each other of sexual relations, unless you both agree to refrain from sexual intimacy for a limited time so you can give yourselves more completely to prayer. Afterward, you should come together again so that Satan won't be able to tempt you because of your lack of self-control. I say this as a concession, not as a command. But I wish everyone were single, just as I am. Yet each person has a special gift from God, of one kind or another.

"So I say to those who aren't married and to widows—it's better to stay unmarried, just as I am. But if they can't control themselves, they should go ahead and marry. It's better to marry than to burn with lust."

~ 1 Corinthians 7:1–9

"For this reason a man will leave his father and mother and be joined to his wife, and they will become one flesh."

~ Genesis 2:24 (NASB)

PROMISES

"'For I know the plans I have for you,' declares the Lord, 'plans to prosper you and not to harm you, plans to give you hope and a future.'"

~ Jeremiah 29:11 (NIV)

"Let us not become weary in doing good, for at the proper time we will reap a harvest if we do not give up."

~ Galatians 6:9 (NIV)

"See, I have written your name on the palms of my hand."

~ Isaiah 49:16

"In the wilderness He fed you manna which your fathers did not know, that He might humble you and that He might test you, to do good for you in the end."

~ Deuteronomy 8:16 (NASB)

"Seek his will in all you do, and he will show you which path to take."

~ Proverbs 3:6

"Trust in the Lord with all your heart and lean not on your own understanding; in all your ways submit to him, and he will make your paths straight."

~ Proverbs 3:5–6 (NIV)

DO

"Jesus said to the people who believed in him, 'You are truly my disciples if you remain faithful to my teachings. And you will know the truth, and the truth will set you free.'"

~ John 8:31–32

"Wait for the Lord; be strong and take heart and wait for the Lord."

~ Psalm 27:14 (NIV)

"Do not add to what I command you and do not subtract from it, but keep the commands of the LORD your God that I give you."

~ Deuteronomy 4:2 (NIV)

"Let love and faithfulness never leave you; bind them around your neck, write them on the tablet of your heart."

~ Proverbs 3:3 (NIV)

"But everyone who hears these words of mine and does not put them into practice is like a foolish man who builds his house on sand. The rain came down, the streams rose, and the winds blew and beat against that house, and it fell with a great crash."

~ Matthew 7:26–27 (NIV)

"Do not be yoked together with unbelievers. For what do righteousness and wickedness have in common? Or what fellowship can light have with darkness?"

~ 2 Corinthians 6:14 (NIV)

"Plans fail for lack of counsel, but with many advisers they succeed."

~ Proverbs 15:22 (NIV)

"Whoever walks in integrity walks securely, but he who makes his ways crooked will be found out."

~ Proverbs 10:9 (ESV)

"But seek first his kingdom and his righteousness, and all these things will be given to you as well."

~ Matthew 6:33 (NIV)

"Therefore do not worry about tomorrow, for tomorrow will worry about itself. Each day has enough trouble of its own."

~ Matthew 6:34 (NIV)

"Come back to the place of safety, all you prisoners who still have hope! I promise this very day that I will repay two blessings for each of your troubles."

~ Zechariah 9:12

"Finally, brothers, whatever is true, whatever is noble, whatever is right, whatever is pure, whatever is lovely, whatever is admirable—if anything is excellent or praiseworthy—think about such things."

~ Philippians 4:8 (NIV)

For more information about

Lindsey Holder

&

Waiting While Dating

please visit:

www.lindseyholder.com
lindsey@lindseyholder.com

For more information about
AMBASSADOR INTERNATIONAL
please visit:

www.ambassador-international.com
@AmbassadorIntl
www.facebook.com/AmbassadorIntl